I AM NOT MY OWN

(JUST ASK MY WIFE)

A Surprisingly Deep 42-Day Devotional
from a Funny Man

SCOTT DAVIS

WITH TIM LUKE

LIFESONG PUBLISHING

Published in the United States by Lifesong Publishing
in partnership with Ampelon Publishing.

ISBN: 978-1-7323117-0-1

Printed in the United States of America

Requests for information should be addressed to:
Ampelon Publishing
PO Box 140675
Boise, ID 83714

Cover design by Spencer Watson

10 9 8 7 6 5 4 3 2 1

First Edition

For Donna, who puts up with me far more than even this book describes and still laughs at my humor…or at least tells me when it's not funny. I love you.

CONTENTS

Keep Your Heart With All Diligence

When I attended Liberty University, I sang in a student group that performed throughout the United States and in several other countries. I've always loved travel and people and foods of all kinds, so I was like a pig in slop.

And that's exactly what I ate in American Samoa.

The locals conducted a traditional tribal night and cooked a whole hog, head and all. I think it still had some hair on the carcass when they served it. Most of our group turned up their noses. I just cut around the hair and gnawed away.

They passed around half a coconut filled with a passion fruit concoction. My team knew me as the guy who would try anything. Give it to Scott. It was like the old Life Cereal commercial: "Give to Mikey. He'll try anything. Hey Mikey!"

I now know all of this played into a food addiction that caused me to swell to more than 300 pounds. That may sound like a rationalization, but I think it's a reality. I know my struggles with weight and food were more a product of environment and personal choices than they were genetics. I didn't have a problem with a gene as much as I had a problem with a Jean. My Mama could fry up a mess of pork chops and taters.

More often than not, we are the sum of our individual decisions. That's scary stuff, but the Bible backs it up.

In Proverbs 23:7, wise King Solomon states a man behaves like he thinks. I like the King James translation: "For as he thinketh in his heart, so is he." Even if what we believe about ourselves is not true, our behavior will reflect our belief in that lie. The Bible says Satan is the father of lies, and he uses lies to deceive us into believing wrong thoughts about ourselves, other people, and many other subjects. The Bible also says he comes to steal, kill, and destroy. It says he disguises himself as an angel of light.

The enemy knows his deceptions are effective because we're no different than his first targets. Those of us who struggle with weight control have no trouble understanding why Adam and Eve suffered the Fall over food. Now, obviously, the fruit from the tree of the knowledge of good and evil was merely the object that revealed hearts already tilted away from God. From the very beginning, the enemy of our souls has pursued one basic deception: He wants us to believe that anything other than God will fulfill us.

Of course, if it had been a donut tree, I would've busted hell wide open in the first 60 seconds.

The desire that drove Eve to pluck off the one fruit she wasn't supposed to eat is the same desire that leads you and me to make our own way. Deep down inside, we think we know better than God. It is essential we counter the enemy's lies with truth.

One goal I have for this book is to solidify your confidence in your identity in Christ. If you have surrendered to Christ, you are a child of the living God. Gaining a better understanding of what that means can help you walk through this daily minefield called life. We all need encouragement, and my prayer is that you will use this resource over the next six weeks to develop or continue the habit of a devotional time with the Lord. Just as with my comedy routine, I pull back the curtains of my personal life in these devotionals. I want to be funny, but I also want the content to have depth and I want to be real. I talk a lot about my wife, Donna, our marriage, my struggles with food, and the general mess I make of things.

Each of the six weeks begins with a slightly longer devotional on Sundays to set the stage for that week's readings. I encourage you to read the Scripture passage of the day before reading the devotional. After each devotional are the same two questions and space for you to record your daily thoughts:

- What truth is God communicating to me right now?
- How is God inviting me to respond?

Wise King Solomon also said, "Keep your heart with all diligence, for out of it spring the issues of life" (Proverbs 4:23). My prayer is that you will find this book helpful in doing just that.

Sunday

John 13:1-11

Secure

If I do not wash you, you have no share with me.

John 13:8

I want a dishwasher that will live up to its name.

I want a dishwasher that will actually wash dishes. Not rinse them off—wash them! I don't want to have to spend 15 minutes washing dishes in the sink to get them ready for the dishwasher. I don't want to own a bottle of Dawn. I want to walk from the kitchen table and shove my dishes in the machine and turn it on. I want to be able to put a plate in that dishwasher with a chicken leg stuck on it, and then take it out with no chicken leg in sight. I have yet to find such a machine.

Despite my travails with the dishwasher, I'm so grateful that Jesus Christ doesn't offer partial cleansing. His atonement of our sin is complete, and our position in him is secure. Once we accept Christ's atonement by his work on the Cross and surrender our hearts to him, we are made God's child forever. A heady word in theology is imputation. It means to attribute something to a person. God took our sins and imputed (attributed) them to Jesus' account in an incomprehensible eternal transaction at the Cross. At the same time, God took Christ's sinless, perfect righteousness and imputed it to our account. When God the Father looks upon a believer, all he sees is the righteousness of Christ.

Second Corinthians 5:21 packs a load of spiritual dynamite: "For our sake he made him to be sin who knew no sin, so that in him we might become the righteousness of God." We cannot wrap our finite minds around this truth. It is more expansive than the universe itself. God made his own Son to be sin as he hung on that Cross. This is why Jesus screamed in agony, "Eli, Eli, lema sabachthani," or, "My God, My God, why have you forsaken me?"

Jesus wasn't quoting Psalm 22:1 just so he could fulfill an Old Testament Messianic prophecy. That fulfillment was part of it, but Jesus' exclamation was the sincere cry of the substitutionary Lamb of God. He experienced the weight of all of our sin. He felt the separation from his Father. He experienced hell on that Cross so we wouldn't have to experience eternal separation from God in hell. So when someone accepts God's free gift of salvation, he is forever secure.

Romans 8:38-39 promises that nothing can separate us from such a profound love as that which God has already demonstrated on Calvary. Spiritually, we are in Christ. This status is fixed by God himself. It cannot be altered.

"In him you also, when you heard the word of truth, the gospel of your salvation, and believed in him, were sealed with the promised Holy Spirit, who is the guarantee of our inheritance until we acquire possession of it, to the praise of his glory" (Ephesians 1:13–14, emphasis added).

Jesus himself spoke to our eternal security: "My sheep hear my voice, and I know them, and they follow me. I give them eternal life, and they will never perish, and no one will snatch them out of my hand" (John 10:27–28).

When God's Holy Spirit dwells inside of you, you know it.

How can one know for sure that he or she is a Christian? First, Romans 8:16 says that God's Holy Spirit bears witness to all believers that we are children of God. When God's Holy Spirit dwells inside of you, you know it.

Another proof is a litmus test provided in 1 John 2:3–6: "And by this we know that we have come to know him, if we keep his commandments. Whoever says 'I know him' but does not keep his commandments is a liar, and the truth is not in him, but whoever keeps his word, in him truly the love of God is perfected. By this we may know that we are in him: whoever says he abides in him ought to walk in the same way in which he walked."

If we know God, if we are his child, we will have an inclination and a desire to obey him just as a child obeys his dad. We will consistently walk in obedience. None of this means we will be perfect. In fact, the reason so many believers struggle with the truth of eternal security is because our failings make us feel how short of God we fall.

If we confess our sins, God is faithful and just to forgive us our sins and to cleanse us from all unrighteousness. (1 John 1:9) So even though Christ has eternally cleansed our sin (singular), or our fallen state, we still must address the sins (plural) we all will commit as long as we're wrapped in our flesh.

On the night before his crucifixion, Jesus gave us an object lesson on this truth. He girded himself with a towel and washed his disciples' feet. Peter, ever the impetuous and bold one, refused to let Jesus condescend to touch his nasty feet. "Jesus answered him, 'If I do not wash you, you have no share with me'" (John 13:8).

Jesus essentially said, "I know you don't fully understand this right now, but if you don't let me perform this daily washing, you neither want nor have anything to do with me." Peter responded by asking Jesus to wash his hands and his head, too. He was saying, "I'm all in!" But Jesus said something very telling: "The one who has bathed does not need to wash, except for his feet, but is completely clean" (John 13:10).

Jesus used an illustration of foot washing to teach us all that, even though we're cleansed and eternally secure, we must be vigilant to confess our shortcomings and ask forgiveness to maintain an intimate fellowship with a holy God.

The Lord doesn't see us as wretched sinners anymore, so we shouldn't see ourselves that way. Instead, God calls us his saints because, again, he sees we are in Christ and clothed in his righteousness.

Yet we should never try to transform this marvelous

freedom God gives us into license. We are here on this Earth to glorify God, and we can't do that by willfully sinning. Too often, believers struggle with the truth of our security in Christ—our right-standing before God—because emotion rather than Scripture is our guide. Isn't it victorious to know that when the Holy Spirit convicts us of sin, we can take it to Jesus and confess it—and He promises to cleanse us?

I believe the Bible from Genesis all the way to the maps. It repeatedly reminds us of one simple truth: You're not holding on to him. He's holding on to you.

"And this is the will of him who sent me, that I should lose nothing of all that he has given me, but raise it up on the last day" (John 6:39).

- What truth is God communicating to me right now?

- How is God inviting me to respond?

Monday

Ephesians 1:3-6

The Firstborn Son

So then, whether we live or whether we die, we are the Lord's.

Romans 14:8

I think I'm like most men when it comes to shopping. We like to make a list. Probably not on paper—that sounds like a lot of work. But a mental list. We like to know exactly what we want before we step foot in the store. Twenty minutes, max, in one of three stores—Wal-Mart, Home Depot, or the Bass Pro Shop. That's all we need.

If I'm at Wal-Mart any more than 20 minutes it's because I'm in a wild mood. Sometimes I hide in a clothes rack just for fun. I wait for someone to come rifling through the clothes. When they pull back the hanger in front of me, I pop out my head and scream, "Pick me!"

It's fun scaring people out of their minds in the clothing department. But the truth-in-jest is that we all have a deep longing to belong. Whether we're on the playground, interviewing for a job, or dating, we want someone to pick us. God made us for fellowship and community, and sin shattered our perfect communion with him in the Garden of Eden. God wasn't done with us yet, however. He made a way for us to reconnect in a relationship with him through his Son, Jesus Christ.

Every bit of the credit belongs to God. We were dead in our trespasses before God rescued us. (Ephesians 2:1) Dead people can't do anything. And why did God rescue us? Because he wanted to.

He picked us.

"Blessed be the God and Father of our Lord Jesus Christ, who has blessed us in Christ with every spiritual blessing in the heavenly places, even as he chose us in him before the foundation of the world, that we should be holy and blameless before him. In love he predestined us for adoption to himself as sons through Jesus Christ, according to the purpose of his will" (Ephesians 1:3–5).

Dead people can't do anything. And why did God rescue us? Because he wanted to.

Paul uses this same word for adoption three times in his letter to the Roman church. In this deeply theological epistle, he knew the idea of God adopting us would resonate in Roman culture. The Roman legal system elevated the adoption of sons so that any adopted male—sometimes even as adults—took the place of the firstborn son. He instantly owned all the rights and privileges of being a firstborn son.

This is exactly how Paul portrays everyone whom God chooses to adopt into his family. Whether you're a man or woman, God treats you like the Romans treated their firstborn sons.

"For you did not receive the spirit of slavery to fall back into fear, but you have received the Spirit of adoption as sons, by whom we cry, "Abba! Father" (Romans 8:15)!

Abba means "Daddy" or "Papa." Draw close to your Heavenly Daddy right now and thank him for wanting you long before you wanted him.

- What truth is God communicating to me right now?

- How is God inviting me to respond?

Tuesday

1 PETER 2:9-10

TERMS OF ENDEARMENT

To the saints and faithful brothers in Christ at Colossae.

COLOSSIANS 1:2

OF THE MANY THINGS I don't understand about women, maybe the most confounding is facial expressions. I'm not always good at reading them.

For instance, I've learned that when my wife gets mad at me, her face may scrunch up like she bit into a lemon, but then she'll throw out a term of endearment with a lilt in her voice: "Honey…."

The face and the words don't match. Her words should just say what her face says: "Hey jerk!" It would be so much less confusing. Please, ladies, if you're upset, just be clear that you're upset. If the storm is coming, give us a National Weather Service bulletin rather than making us go outside to try to read the skies. At least then we'll know to duck and cover rather than to blindly walk right into it.

Throughout our lives people have used terms of endearment in speaking to us. Especially in the South, we're used to words like Sweetheart, Sugar, Darling, or Honey. I walked into a store the other day and asked for help. "Sure, Honey!" It was as if she'd known me my whole life.

God has terms of endearment for us as well, but they're not empty greetings. He uses terms like "Sons of the Lord your God" in Deuteronomy 14:1, or "Daughter of Jerusalem" and "Daughter of Zion" in Micah 4:8, 10. In the New Testament, God calls us his "children" in Romans 8:15, "sons and daughters" in 2 Corinthians 6:18, and "saints" in several books. One of my favorite terms of endearment from God is when he says that believers are "God's chosen ones, holy and beloved" (Colossians 3:12).

Ephesians 1:4-5 reminds us that God decided in advance to adopt us into his own family by bringing us to himself through Jesus Christ. He wanted the relationship each believer enjoys with him. It gives him great pleasure to call us his own. His terms of endearment come with no ambiguity, no guessing games.

We know exactly where we stand—in the middle of his grace, a child who belongs to the one true King. We can rejoice in being his today.

- What truth is God communicating to me right now?

- How is God inviting me to respond?

MATTHEW 16:24-26

EXPECTATIONS

So God created man in his own image, in the image of God he created him; male and female he created them.

GENESIS 1:27

GOD LOVES ALL OF US CRAZY, goofy, childish, idiotic men. That's a fact. But he has to love us, because that's what it takes to put up with us crazy, goofy, childish, idiotic men.

And God loves all you wonderful, sweet, beautiful... convinced-you're-correct...women. In fact, I thank the Lord that I married Ms. Right. I just didn't know her first name was Always.

Today's society has placed a lot of expectations on both men and women. Modern American culture dictates that we should strive for prominence in education, the workplace, politics, and so on. The world coaxes all of us to correlate our value with achievements in these arenas.

Each of those pursuits can be worthy. However, when what we do becomes who we are—when our identities are rooted in money, careers, titles, and success—we're headed for heartbreak. I heard a minister at my church say that when our identity is not found in Christ, we go around like beggars, holding out our cup for others to fill as we seek love, acceptance, worth, and security. But that cup has a hole in it. We always need someone else to try to fill it again.

Jesus saved his most intimate advice for his closest friends, the disciples. In one instance, he told them, "If anyone would come after me, let him deny himself and take up his cross and follow me. For whoever would save his life will lose it, but whoever loses his life for my sake will find it. For what will it profit a man if he gains the whole world and forfeits his soul? Or what shall a man give in return for his soul" (Matthew 16:24-26)?

Never determine your value by what you do or achieve in this world. Never let the opinions of others rule your life. Base your value only in your identity in Christ, the one who purchased you with his blood. To him alone do you belong.

The Bible tells me that Jesus purchased me with his shed blood and that I am not my own. My wife likes to remind me how much I belong to her too, especially when it's time to cut the grass or wash dishes. I'm tempted to mutter, "You're not the boss of me," but I'm thankful for her and wouldn't have it any other way.

First Corinthians 6:19-20 states, "You are not your own, for you were bought with a price." That means God has placed a rightful claim on our lives. He has saved our souls from damnation and has the right to use what he has bought as he sees fit.

Both men and women bear the image of God, and we are all sinners equally in need of his saving grace (Galatians 3:28). The prophet Jeremiah reminds us where to put our focus:

> This is what the LORD says:

"Don't let the wise boast in their wisdom,
or the powerful boast in their power,
or the rich boast in their riches.
But those who wish to boast
should boast in this alone:
that they truly know me and understand
that I am the LORD
who demonstrates unfailing love
and who brings justice and righteousness to the earth,
and that I delight in these things.
I, the LORD, have spoken! (Jeremiah 9:23-24)

The Lord has spoken: We should concern ourselves only with his expectations, not those of other people, and should focus our hearts on the one true satisfier of our souls—Jesus.

- What truth is God communicating to me right now?

- How is God inviting me to respond?

Thursday

1 Peter 5:6-11

Airs

Humble yourselves, therefore, under the mighty hand of God so that at the proper time he may exalt you.

1 Peter 5:6

Men will make up stuff around women. I don't care if we're married, single, divorced, widowed, whatever—if there is a member of the opposite sex anywhere around, we men cannot possibly act like we don't know what we're doing. At all costs, we have to save face.

Someone may ask, "Have you ever bungee jumped?"

The man glances at the nearest woman and says, "I do that three times a week."

"Have you ever jumped out of an airplane?"

"Well, that's how I used to go to work. Before I bought my helicopter."

Whatever it takes to impress, we just make it up.

The good news of the gospel is that in God's eyes we have nothing to prove, no one to impress. Think about it: How could we possibly make an impression on an infinite, holy God anyway?

No creature is hidden from God's sight, but all are naked and exposed to the eyes of him to whom we must give account (Hebrews 4:13). Since God sees our hearts and knows all of our motives, why should we ever put on airs or do anything but live authentic lives before him and others?

Putting on airs is trying to achieve temporal approval from man. Deep down, we recognize our shortcomings, and our insecurity drives us to profess to be someone we're not.

Galatians 6 features a passage that should make us think. "Do not be deceived: God is not mocked, for whatever one sows, that will he also reap. For the one who sows to his own flesh will from the flesh reap corruption, but the one who sows to the Spirit will from the Spirit reap eternal life" (vv. 7–8).

God does not value what man values. He does not reward what man rewards.

God does not value what man values. He does not reward what man rewards. We all can learn from the Apostle Paul's example. When chastising the Corinthian church, he reminded them that he was weak and held in disrepute. He said he was hungry, thirsty, poorly dressed, buffeted, and homeless. He said he had become, and still was at the moment he wrote the letter, "like the scum of the world, the refuse of all things" (1 Corinthians 4:10-13).

We don't necessarily need to sell our homes and become vagabonds to preach Christ, but we can live crucified lives too. We can die to our flesh and our insatiable urges to impress and to accumulate status and wealth. We can go back to Galatians 6 and be more like Paul: "But far be it from me to boast except in the cross of our Lord Jesus Christ, by which the world has been crucified to me, and I to the world" (Galatians 6:14).

- What truth is God communicating to me right now?

- How is God inviting me to respond?

Friday

2 Corinthians 5:17 & John 19:38-42

Before and After

You are not your own, for you were bought with a price.

1 Corinthians 6:19-20

I never trust advertisements with before-and-after photos. I'm convinced some of them show two different people. Here's Tubby before. Here's Thomas afterward. Perhaps Tubby and Thomas are brothers separated at birth, but they ain't the same dude.

In other ads, a grainy candid photo shows an overweight lady at a family reunion, mouth full of egg salad and wearing something that looks like either a maternity blouse or a hot air balloon. In the next photo, somebody who doesn't come close to resembling Reunion Girl is posing in spandex shorts and a sports bra showing off her shredded abs. And she did it in six weeks! Umm…don't think so.

Other examples include photos clearly of the same man, but in the Before photo he's a little meaty and in the After photo he's sucking in his gut so far that his navel touches his spine. I have a rule: Don't trust the photo if you can see someone's entire bottom rib.

The only Before-and-After I trust is God's. He alone can transform us so completely that our new lives are unrecognizable even to the people who love us most. During more than three decades in ministry, I have seen God's miraculous touch in lives all over the world.

One of my favorite conversion stories is traced throughout the book of John. The third chapter of the book introduces Nicodemus, a member of the ruling Sanhedrin. John 3:16 is perhaps the most familiar verse in the entire Bible, and Nicodemus was the first lost man to hear it. Nicodemus' questions show he is sincerely intrigued by Jesus.

By the time Nicodemus shows up again in John 7, he has the courage to defend Jesus in a procedural matter (vv. 50-52).

Even the name Nicodemus meant "innocent blood."

Finally, in John 19:38-42, we see Nicodemus as a sold-out devotee to his new Lord as he wraps and buries the body of his crucified Savior. The blood of Jesus literally covered him in an act that would have made him not only unclean but also excommunicated from the Temple. Even the name Nicodemus means "innocent blood."

Radical change marked Nicodemus. His faith in Christ made him abandon everything he held dear, everything that gave him station in life. It's not the story of a superhero Bible character. It's the story of Jesus changing a heart tilted away from him.

Remember when Jesus changed you? Whom will you commit to pray for Jesus to change next?

- What truth is God communicating to me right now?

- How is God inviting me to respond?

Saturday

1 JOHN 5:1-12

THAT YOU MAY KNOW

Everyone who believes that Jesus is the Christ has been born of God.

1 JOHN 5:1

SOMETIMES I THINK MY WIFE wants me to change my name to Zofar the Incredible. For some reason, I'm supposed to know exactly what she's thinking and what she wants me to do at all times.

I have to tell her, "Don't expect me to be a mind reader." Sometimes I think it's because women are so much more intuitive than men that they think we men are just dumb. Yet for men, life is all about convenience and having the right tool. If we have the right tool, we can do anything. The extent of our thought process is, "See problem, attack problem."

I've learned that women aren't necessarily wired that way. If marriage vows reflected true marriage life, instead of the women saying, "I do," they'd make us guess the answer.

I'm glad that we don't have to guess when it comes to our personal relationship with Christ. We can know that we have eternal life. That claim can be offensive. Sometimes people who don't know God are put off by anyone who claims he is certain he will go to heaven. They think it's the height of arrogance to claim to know God personally. Ironically, it is their own pride that is keeping them from knowing the only God there is to know.

The Apostle John writes, "I write these things to you who believe in the name of the Son of God, that you may know that you have eternal life" (1 John 5:13). It's so simple that we could almost miss it, but knowing that we belong to God comes from believing in Jesus. This is the heart of the gospel. When we trust in his name—and his name represents his eternal, perfect, and trustworthy character—we stop trying to earn heaven by being moral. Instead, we depend on his righteousness imputed to us when Christ took our place on the Cross.

When we trust in his name, we stop trying to earn heaven by being moral.

My assurance does not depend on how much I've done or how well I did it but on whether I rest in Christ's finished work on the Cross. When we consider all that Christ has done to facilitate our salvation and is the one who worked in our hearts to convict us to surrender our lives to him, it is a statement of humility, not arrogance, to say we know him.

The word *believe* in John 3:16 is the Greek word *pisteuo* and means "to trust," and it carries the connotation of placing all of your weight on the object of your trust. When you sit in a chair, you pisteuo that chair—you place all of your weight on it and don't even give it a second thought as you completely trust it to bear your weight. Have you placed all of your weight, for now and eternity, on Jesus?

You don't have to play a guessing game. "I write these things to you who believe in the name of the Son of God, that you may *know* that you have eternal life."

- What truth is God communicating to me right now?

- How is God inviting me to respond?

Sunday

Isaiah 55:8-9

Rounded Edges

"For my thoughts are not your thoughts, neither are your ways my ways," declares the LORD.

Isaiah 55:8

I try to pitch in and do my share of chores around the house. When Donna is cleaning house, I make sure I help her….

Usually…

Sometimes…

When she makes me.

Not long ago, we tackled the laundry and I started out by folding towels because it's easy. I bargained with Donna a little to make myself look good: "You wash the clothes, and I'll fold." I began folding and feeling good about myself—it's a towel; how can you mess up a towel, right? I've always been a confident towel folder, and in no time, I finished folding my first towel in a perfect square and plopped it down. Why a square? Because it's a towel!

That's when Donna looked over her shoulder. She doesn't have eyes in the back of her head, but I'm pretty sure she has cameras everywhere.

"Honey…" she said.

Uh-oh. Another term of endearment.

"That's not how you fold a towel," she said.

I answered her the only way I knew how: "It's a towel."

She unfolded my towel and launched into her tutorial on how to fold a towel according to her personal algorithm. "It's a third here and a third there and another third here." She lost me when she said the word "third."

But I did notice that her finished towel had a beautiful round end—like the kind you see on a department store shelf.

"Ooh!" I said, "That'll slide in the linen closet easy. We can just slide the rounded end in first and wedge it right in there."

Donna shook her head.

"No way. The rounded edge has to show on the outside."

"Why?"

"Because that's the pretty side."

Now I was really stumped.

"As if I'm going to invite someone over, give them the grand tour, and swing open the closet door and say, 'By the way, here's my lovely linen closet. Don't we have beautiful towels? Don't you like those rounded edges? Reminds you of Bed, Bath, and Beyond, doesn't it?'"

I give Donna credit for doing things with excellence, however. Order is not natural. When I think of my house, I'm shocked at how fast order can fall into chaos—even with little things like folding or not folding towels. With some effort, we can bring order to our physical lives, but we cannot bring order to the emotional and spiritual chaos of our lives. Only Christ can do that.

No sentence in human history is more full of meaning than Genesis 1:1. "In the beginning, God created the heavens and the earth." It means God created all matter ex nihilo, Latin for "out of nothing." He made something from nothing. The first (very short) sentence in the Bible presents several facts:

1) God is eternal, had no creator, and created all things. 2) As Pastor Derek Thomas writes for Ligonier Ministries, nothing existed apart from God and everything that exists apart from God was brought into existence by him.[1] 3) God had no helper and needed none. Everything that was done was done by the one true God.

God created an earth that was formless and void (Genesis 1:2). He still had some shaping to do. And look how beautiful it is now.

God created you, too (Psalm 139:13-16), and is still at work shaping and molding you. Though you once were dead spiritually, you now are a new creature in Christ, a beautiful new creation ex nihilo.

As the Lord shapes and molds you through his Word and Holy Spirit, he rounds your corners and brings order to your chaos when you cannot. "The heart of man plans his way, but the LORD establishes his steps" (Proverbs 16:9). Romans 11:33-34 tells us that God's wisdom is too deep and unsearchable for the human mind and uses the word "inscrutable" to describe God's ways. Inscrutable is another word for unfathomable. The way God thinks and orchestrates cannot be fully comprehended by our finite minds.

Isaiah 55:8-9 says it in plain language. "For my thoughts are not your thoughts, neither are your ways my ways, declares the LORD. For as the heavens are higher than the earth, so are my ways higher than your ways and my thoughts than your thoughts."

It's clear that not much beyond folding our proverbial towels is within our control. We are left to trust or not trust. Believe or not believe. Whatever circumstances in which you find yourself right now, are you still trying to make sure the rounded edges are facing outward? Are you trying to control everything—for appearances if nothing else?

Stop striving. Let go.

"Trust in the LORD with all your heart, and do not lean on your own understanding. In all your ways acknowledge Him, and He will make your paths straight" (Proverbs 3:5-6).

Only God can straighten the wrinkles of the spiritual chaos in our lives—when we live as he intends and simply trust him.

- What truth is God communicating to me right now?

- How is God inviting me to respond?

Monday

Joshua 1:7-9

Fear Itself

Do not be frightened, and do not be dismayed, for the LORD your God is with you wherever you go.

Joshua 1:9

On a recent doctor's visit, I realized just how bored I get when I'm left to myself. As I waited in the exam room, I noticed the tall glass jar that seems to be in every doctor's office. It contains wide, flat sticks used as tongue depressors.

I couldn't resist. I popped open the jar and started playing with them. I tried building a stick house but realized I didn't have any glue. After a few minutes, I used them to press down my tongue and say, "Ahhhhh" in the mirror. And then I put them back in the jar.

I was afraid the doctor would walk in and find me doing something stupid, and he did. He stepped into the room as I sat in the corner chair and played drums with the few remaining sticks I hadn't licked. They worked great on the trashcan with the foot pedal for the lid. He came in right after I heard the lady in the next room scream. She was probably having her pacemaker checked when she heard Van Halen crank up next door.

As silly as that story sounds, many times when we are

facing something unknown, like at a doctor's office, fear can creep into our hearts. It sounds trite, but it remains an absolute truth: Christ is with us and doesn't want us to worry or fear! God does not give believers a spirit of fear but instead, through his Holy Spirit, a spirit of power, love, and self-control (2 Timothy 1:7). Since the spirit of fear does not come from God, we can deduce that it comes from Satan, the destroyer who wishes to neutralize God's children through fear and worry.

In only the fifth sentence of his 1933 inaugural address, President Franklin D. Roosevelt stared into the cavernous depths of The Great Depression and told a frightened country a great truth: "The only thing we have to fear is fear itself—nameless, unreasoning, unjustified terror which paralyzes needed efforts to convert retreat into advance."[2] He knew how debilitating fear and worry become as they fuel each other. Yet Roosevelt was only talking about a devastated economy. In our spiritual economy, the stakes are much higher. They impact eternity. In our efforts to advance God's Kingdom, we often face nameless, unreasoning, unjustified terror—nothing but fear itself, and it paralyzes. The enemy knows that if he can weigh down our hearts with the cast-iron shackles of fear, we will worry ourselves into doing nothing for God's glory.

Scripture answers with Philippians 4:6. "Do not be anxious about anything, but in everything by prayer and supplication with thanksgiving let your requests be made known to God. And the peace of God, which surpasses all understanding, will guard your hearts and your minds in Christ Jesus."

The verses preceding verse 6 offer the antidote for fear and worry: Rejoice in the Lord and let your reasonableness be known to everyone. In other words, rejoice in the fact that you know God through his Son, Jesus Christ, and everything else pales in that unapproachable light. What have you to worry about when you already know your ultimate outcome? So be reasonable about your situation. Balance it against Scripture and trust God for the results.

- What truth is God communicating to me right now?

- How is God inviting me to respond?

Tuesday

JOHN 14:16-17

YOU ARE NOT ALONE

You know him, for he dwells with you and will be in you.

JOHN 14:17

MARK LOWRY, THE CHRISTIAN COMEDIAN and member of the Gaither Vocal Band, is an old college buddy. He owns a pair of antique beds that are more than 100 years old that were a gift from singer Michael English. Years ago, in my heavier days, I wound up sleeping on one of those antiques when I visited Mark.

I tossed and turned like a lot of big people do, and the ancient bed creaked and cracked under my weight. It kept me awake in an endless cycle. I'd turn over, and the bed would creak and pop and wake me up, which made me toss and turn even more. I was starting to worry that I was keeping up everybody in the house when—boom!— the bed seemed to explode as it thudded to the floor.

In the middle of the night.

In an expensive bed.

In a famous person's home.

One end of the bed frame collapsed, making a horrible racket and leaving one end of the bed on the floor and the other still connected to the frame. I waited a few moments with one eye half open, but no one else stirred.

I was too lazy to get up, so I just slept uphill the rest of the night.

Not only have I broken a bed before, but I've also destroyed a rickety chair or two. I've struggled with my weight most of my life, and these embarrassing moments reminded me I needed to do something about it. My wife and friends would prod me to do something, and I answered with empty promises, usually cutting my eyes back to the buffet line.

Aren't you glad that God's promises are more trustworthy than anything or anyone on this earth? God means what he says and follows through on his Word. I take solace in God's promise in Hebrews 13:5: "I will never leave you nor forsake you." The beautiful part of that promise is that the writer of Hebrews takes the quote from when God encouraged Joshua as he took over leadership of the Israelites from Moses. Yet the Lord saw fit to leave every single New Testament believer with the same promise he issued one of his greatest leaders.

God means what he says and follows through on his Word.

"I will never leave you nor forsake you."

Just as God was with Joshua when he faced a whole new land and its frightening inhabitants, he is with you and me as we face a whole new day. Whatever lies ahead, you are not alone. Even when you wake up in a broken bed.

- What truth is God communicating to me right now?

- How is God inviting me to respond?

Wednesday

John 14:20-24

The Driver's Seat

Whoever has my commandments and keeps them, he it is who loves me.

John 14:21

If I'm going to ride in a car, I have to drive. It's a control thing. When you're the driver, you're like the captain of the car. You rule over everything in that car. People. Air conditioner. Radio. All of it is your domain.

You can control everyone's windows. You can decide where to eat. You can tell somebody, "Buckle your seat belt" and not come off as a jerk because the driver just has that power—unless you're 16 and driving your dad around town. My dad never would buckle his seat belt. He always said that in a wreck he wanted to be thrown clear. I said, "Sit on the hood. You can bypass the windshield that way." He didn't like that.

As much as we'd like to get people to change and do what is right, we can't change anybody. Only God can renew a person. It saddens me to see people not living biblically, but the flip side is also true. We all have blind spots, and sometimes my friends have had to point out something in my life that wasn't Christlike as well. Believers should live according to Christ's commands and teachings, allowing the Holy Spirit to take the driver's seat of our lives and let Christ live through us in front of others. Those old car tags that read, "Jesus is My Co-Pilot" are well intentioned but get on my nerves. Jesus isn't our co-pilot. If we're walking with him, he has total control and we offer total submission.

We should live in such a way that people know we're followers of Jesus. If over time they're unclear about who we are and what we believe, then we're frauds. We should make biblical truths clear to others in a loving way, but then we must leave it up to God to effect the changes of the heart.

We should live in such a way that people know we're followers of Jesus.

In the Old Testament, God promised what he would do through his New Covenant: "And I will give you a new heart, and a new spirit I will put within you. And I will remove the heart of stone from your flesh and give you a heart of flesh. And I will put my Spirit within you, and cause you to walk in my statutes and be careful to obey my rules" (Ezekiel 36:26–27). The duty of the believer is to live and speak in such a way that our allegiance to Jesus has no ambiguity. Really, the only thing we control is whether we will obey.

Let's love and live as Christ would and trust him with the consequences in our lives and in the lives of others.

- What truth is God communicating to me right now?

- How is God inviting me to respond?

Thursday

John 6:1-14

God Is Not Cheap

Gather up the leftover fragments, that nothing may be lost.

John 6:12

My wife is classy, classy, classy—first class all the way. She likes the finest of things. Not that I'm low-class. I'm just junky. Like, salvage-yard junky. Sanford-and-Son junky.

That's another way of saying I'm cheap.

I have to admit that I can squeeze the wax out of Abe's ears on a penny. My wife likes to shop at big department stores in Atlanta's huge malls. Me? Everything on my body right now has a "Faded Glory" tag on it. If you're not sure what that is, go peruse a few clothing racks at Wal-Mart. If Suave would make a car, I'd drive it.

But I'm so glad God is not cheap.

John 2:1-11 details the story of Jesus turning water into wine at a wedding in the small town of Cana in Galilee. The house hosting the wedding feast has six stone water jars for purification rites. They hold between 20 and 30 gallons each. That's up to 180 gallons of water that Jesus turns into wine. Seeing as how Jesus wouldn't willingly provide for people to get drunk, there must've been a huge crowd at the wedding. Also, keep in mind that weddings in ancient Israel lasted for a week. The whole town was involved.

Nevertheless, the average serving of wine is five ounces, which means Jesus provides more than 4,500 servings of wine by speaking them into existence. In other words, Jesus supplies more than enough.

Later in John (6:1-14), we find another example of God's lavish grace for physical needs. Jesus takes a small boy's five loaves of bread and two fish and miraculously multiplies them to feed 5,000 men and their families—likely a crowd of at least 15,000 people. Afterwards the disciples collect 12 baskets of leftovers. Again, he provides more than enough.

These examples show God's willingness to meet our needs with some to spare. Stop for a moment and think how the Lord has provided for you and your loved ones throughout your life. Thank him for his graciousness. Let gratitude replace any worry or concern you may have over your current circumstances or the future. God has proven himself faithful to you, has he not?

But don't limit God to barely meeting your needs. When we trust him and he gives us more than we need, he does it so we can bless and meet the needs of others! He leads by example and expects us to follow him in generosity and faithfulness. Don't pray for God to help and bless others. YOU help and bless others in his name. Be the answer to your own prayer for them.

So, trust Jesus. His grace is not cheap, and neither is he.

- What truth is God communicating to me right now?

- How is God inviting me to respond?

Friday

ROMANS 8:28-39

GOD LOVES SHORT PEOPLE

For those whom he foreknew he also predestined to be conformed to the image of his Son.

ROMANS 8:29

A COUPLE OF MY FRIENDS are identical twins whose names are Rick and Mick. They're about 5-foot-4. They're small in stature but huge in personality and sense of humor. They'll quickly tell you that God loves short people because Jesus promises in the Bible, "Lo, I am with you always."

They cracked that joke to me, and I couldn't resist. I had to remind them that the Bible also says the wicked shall be cut off.

I'm thankful that I have a lot of friends who love to laugh and joke. Some are short like Rick and Mick; others are bald. Some are overweight, and some look like magazine models. No matter who we are, we're all beautiful in God's eyes, regardless of what anyone else says.

Growing up, I was always the "husky" boy. That was the polite way of saying I was fat. Sometimes kids made fun of me. I discovered that adolescent years in particular can be tough. Much of my life I was self-conscious about my appearance and told myself I needed to physically change certain features and shortcomings. I wasn't mature enough in any way, including spiritually, to know the truth of my identity in Christ, the truth of how God sees me.

I'm not saying we shouldn't be the best we can be physically, but as I've aged I've learned to tune out negative voices and replace them with God's Word. One of the pleasures of constantly soaking in Scripture is the contentment of learning his promises and applying them to our lives. It is life-changing to commit truth to your heart and be able to recall it in low moments or times of need. You can't claim God's promises if you don't know them.

It is life-changing to commit truth to your heart and be able to recall it in low moments or times of need.

For instance, Scripture tells me I am the apple of God's eye (Psalm 17:8)! As a friend of mine says, "God is crazy about me." And he is about you too!

Psalms 139 shows us how intimately God knows us: "You created every part of me; you put me together in my mother's womb....When my bones were being formed, carefully put together in my mother's womb, when I was growing there in secret, you knew that I was there—you saw me before I was born" (vv. 13, 15-16, Good News Translation). And yet Romans 8 tells us nothing can separate us from the love of God in Christ Jesus.

The Bible says you are created in God's image, which means that you have a special place in his heart. You are loved, you have a purpose, and you are not a mistake!

Rick and Mick would tell you that's the long and short of it.

- What truth is God communicating to me right now?

- How is God inviting me to respond?

Saturday

PHILIPPIANS 4:10-20

WHAT ARE YOU CHASING?

For I have learned in whatever situation I am to be content.

PHILIPPIANS 4:11

I LIKE GADGETS. And I like buying stuff—not necessarily going shopping, but buying stuff. When you like gadgets, and you like to buy things, that's a dangerous combination.

Years ago, I bought the voice-activated TV remote control before they became popular on many models. I speak into the remote's microphone, and it changes channels. I'll say, "Channel Five!" and it goes straight to Channel Five. It has a glitch though, especially when the TV is too loud. The nightly news teaser will come on and say, "Tonight at 11…" and, poof, it changes to Channel Eleven. Drives me crazy.

I usually tell it to take me to the Home Shopping Network. If you're ever up at 2 a.m., flip over there and you might just hear the hushed baritone voice of "Scott from Stockbridge" tell the host, "I just love that broach."

I can't resist buying their silly stuff either. I bought a cow telephone. When the phone rings it sounds like a cow. We get a call at the house, and my mouth waters because I think I hear a Chick-Fil-A commercial: Moooooo…moooooo…
.mooooo.

I won't even tell you what it does when you put it on hold, but it's amazing.

I'm enamored with the latest and greatest. Even if I don't buy it, I'm interested. Did you hear about the new doll on the market? It's called Divorced Barbie. It comes with half of Ken's stuff.

Paul is telling us to trust God in all circumstances.

I probably shouldn't joke about divorce, but I'm laughing at my own track record of getting caught up in materialism. I don't buy expensive stuff; I just buy too much stuff. I buy things I don't really need.

The Apostle Paul gives us a good example concerning needs and wants. Somehow, we've taken what he said and used it in the wrong context far too often. He tells the Philippians church, "I can do all things through him who strengthens me" (4:13). We often see this verse used in sports and in other circumstances where people are overachieving. That's not what Paul meant at all.

He was saying just the opposite. Paul wrote this statement while in prison. He intended it as a statement of faith during the lowest of moments—when his gut gnawed in hunger and his body ached in sickness and the sores on his back oozed after yet another beating. It has nothing to do with the idea that God will bless whatever we choose to do. It has nothing to do with winning a championship and beaming into the camera.

"I have learned in whatever situation I am to be content. I know how to be brought low, and I know how to abound. In any and every circumstance, I have learned the secret of facing plenty and hunger, abundance and need" (Philippians 4:11–12).

And only then does he add, "I can do all things through Him who strengthens me."

Paul is telling us to trust God in all circumstances. Are you content today? What are you chasing? Is your eye on anything other than Christ to fulfill you? When you are at your lowest, are you willing to confess that you can do and bear all things through the God who longs to be your only source of strength?

- What truth is God communicating to me right now?

- How is God inviting me to respond?

Sunday

GENESIS 16:1-13

GOD KNOWS AND CARES

The angel of the LORD *found her by a spring of water in the wilderness ...*

GENESIS 16:7

AFTER BEING MARRIED to a nurse for 20 years, I've learned a universal truth the hard way: Nurses have no sympathy whatsoever…

For their spouses.

Nurses are wonderful with their patients and other people. They'll wade into someone else's blood and gaping wounds and all manner of stressful mayhem and not think twice. But let their closest loved one need a little TLC, and watch what happens.

Nothing. Nothing happens.

Unless I have a limb missing and blood squirting to the ceiling, Donna won't bother to look my way. If I had a chainsaw accident, my wife would roll her eyes, and I know what I'd hear.

"You're fine. You'll get over it."

"But it's hanging by a thread!"

"Just shake it off."

If we're honest, sometimes it feels that way with God. When it seems life is imploding and hope is a faint, abstract idea, it's easy to think, "Nobody knows what I'm going through, nobody feels the pain I'm experiencing."

Even King David was transparent enough to admit that he experienced times of feeling God had abandoned him. "How long, O Lord? Will you forget me forever? How long will you hide your face from me? How long must I take counsel in my soul and have sorrow in my heart all the day" (Psalm 13:1-2)?

The Christian walk engages the emotions, but it cannot be based on emotions. It must be based on the infallible truths of God's Word. And this is what Scripture says about whatever struggle you now face:

God knows.

The same David who lamented feeling God's absence in Psalm 13 also reminds himself of God's trustworthiness in Psalm 32. He even writes this assurance in such a way that it reminds us that God does indeed see. He sees the crisis or heartache that burdens you. David records a promise God spoke to him at a low point. "I will instruct you and teach you in the way you should go. I will counsel you with my eye upon you" (Psalm 32:8).

The truth that God sees us intimately is threaded throughout Scripture. One of the first places it is revealed is in Genesis in an unlikely context—the story of the servant girl Hagar.

Even though Abram and Sarah were old, God promises them a son whose many descendants will become the nation Israel. In their impatience for God to honor his word, the elderly couple takes matters into their own hands. Sarah hatches a plan for Abram to conceive a child with her Egyptian handmaiden, Hagar. As human nature goes, this arrangement creates great conflict. As soon as Hagar is pregnant—something for which Sarah has longed for years—the prideful young Hagar has contempt for Sarah.

Sarah retaliates against Hagar, who flees to the wilderness. There, the Angel of the Lord meets her by a spring of water and reassures her. He tells her that she will bear a son and to return to Sarah. With a new plan for her life planted firmly in her heart, Hagar pronounces a new name for God: El-Roi (El-Row-EE). It means "the God who sees." Hagar knew God had seen her desperation and responded to her cries.

But the story doesn't end there. Hagar says something illuminating for all of us after calling God El-Roi. In her next breath, she says, "Truly here I have seen him who looks after me" (Genesis 16:13). First, Hagar realizes that God sees her. Then she says, "I have seen him." In one passage of Scripture, Hagar acknowledges that after God first sees her, she then clearly can see him moving in her life. She learns the tremendous catalyst of faith.

This episode in Genesis is the first recorded appearance of the Angel of the Lord. Notice the capital A in Angel. This Angel appears several times in the Old Testament, and most scholars believe it is a theophany—a literal appearance of God. More precisely, the Angel of the Lord is considered to be a pre-incarnate appearance of Christ. Hagar knows who had visited her, and some commentators have concluded that the name Hagar uses for God actually means The God Who Sees Me. Perhaps even more intimately, it can also be translated The God Who Sees After Me.

The same God whom Hagar says looks after us is the same Jesus who says in Matthew 10:30 that even the hairs of our heads are numbered. The Lord not only knows your circumstances but also your feelings and frustrations. He knows your suffering and fear. No hurt goes unnoticed by Him.

He knows your suffering and fear. No hurt goes unnoticed by Him.

Psalm 56:8-11 assures us: "You have kept count of my tossings; put my tears in your bottle. Are they not in your book?... This I know, that God is for me. In God, whose word I praise, in the LORD, whose word I praise, in God I trust; I shall not be afraid. What can man do to me?"

We often feel isolated and lonely when we're hurting. Maybe you've had a death in the family, a divorce, or maybe you've lost a job. Maybe you or a loved one struggles with addiction. It's easy to think, "Nobody understands the way I feel; nobody feels my pain."

But take heart. God knows.

"The LORD is like a father to his children, tender and compassionate to those who fear him" (Psalm 103:13).

Rest in the truth that the one true God watches over you. In faith trust him that he sees you and in his timing will move in such a way that you will come to see him and the depth of his love in a way that you never have before.

El-Roi is with you. He sees.

- What truth is God communicating to me right now?

- How is God inviting me to respond?

Monday

MATTHEW 10:34-39

DO YOU LOVE GOD LIKE THAT?

And whoever does not take his cross and follow me is not worthy of me.

MATTHEW 10:38

AS A CARD-CARRYING MEMBER of the male gender, I can honestly say I love to sleep. I think most men do. I'm pretty sure our DNA stands for Do Not Awake. Some days it's just difficult to get up and go to work.

However, we men will get up at 4 a.m. in the middle of winter and slog through the deepest woods to sit in a deer stand, and we won't think twice about it. We'll freeze our rear ends off until we find something to shoot. If we don't shoot something in the woods, we'll shoot something on the way home just for therapy.

"Where's that cat?" Boom!

Kidding. Sorry. I don't condone shooting cats.

Usually.

Isn't it interesting that when we really love something, we'll make time for it? Men who love hunting will get out of a warm bed at unnatural hours to do what they love. If one of our children is sick in the middle of the night, we'll rise without a concern for ourselves and make sure they're OK.

Now, what if we all approached our relationship with

Jesus the same way? What if we truly loved Jesus more than anyone else in our lives?

When I was younger, I was puzzled by a passage in Matthew. I knew Jesus was talking because the words were in red: "Whoever loves father or mother more than me is not worthy of me, and whoever loves their son or daughter more than me is not worthy of me" (Matthew 10:37).

I loved my parents and grandparents so much that it was hard to grasp loving someone more than I loved them. As I've matured and fallen in love with Jesus through his Word and his Holy Spirit's ministry in my life, I've come to understand what he means in this passage. I have grown to love him more than life itself.

Later, Jesus is asked to name the greatest commandment. He goes right back to love for himself. "'Love the Lord your God with all your heart and with all your soul and with all your mind,'" he says (Matthew 22:37).

I looked up the word *all* in the dictionary. I figured since it was such a little word, it would say, "all means all and that's all that all means." But it didn't. It says, "The whole of; the whole number of; ...wholly; entirely; completely."[3]

The Bible teaches we should love God with all that we are and everything we have, completely consumed in Him. Do you love God like that? We make time for what we really love.

"And whoever does not take his cross and follow me is not worthy of me. Whoever finds his life will lose it, and whoever loses his life for my sake will find it" (John 10:38-39).

- What truth is God communicating to me right now?

- How is God inviting me to respond?

Tuesday

2 Timothy 3:14-17

Expiration

And how from childhood you have been acquainted with the sacred writings, which are able to make you wise for salvation through faith in Christ Jesus.
2 Timothy 3:15

I struggle with sleep apnea, which is not really a laughing matter. It's where you stop breathing for long periods of time while you sleep, and you wake up gasping for air.

I've never been able to wear the CPAP mask my doctor prescribed. It forces positive air pressure through my airway to help me breathe, but I don't tolerate it well. One morning I woke up gasping for air at 3 a.m. and looked over at my beautiful wife, who happens to be a nurse, and she was holding up her wrist to look at her watch.

"You went a minute and a half and didn't breathe," she said.

"Well, when were you going to poke me?" I said. "Two minutes? Five minutes? When I was blue?"

I told a friend about the episode. "Yeah, she was counting all right," he said. "She was counting life insurance money."

Here's the thing: I learned a long time ago that God's breath is more important than mine. The Greek word for "breath" is *pneuma*, which also can be translated as "spirit" or "wind." In John 3:8, when Jesus is talking to Nicodemus about the work of the Holy Spirit in salvation, he says, "The wind (*pneuma*) blows where it wishes." Just as we don't understand how the wind blows, we also can't fathom how God's Spirit works.

Second Timothy 3:16 holds that all Scripture is *theopneust*. The first part of that Greek word, *theo*, means God. The second part of the word is a derivation of *pneuma* that means "breathed." So all Scripture is God-breathed. Some Bible versions translate the word *theopneust* as "inspiration," so that all Scripture is given by "inspiration" of God.

Pastor R. C. Sproul taught that a better translation of the word *theopneust* is "expiration" rather than "inspiration."

"When (Paul) insists that all of the Scripture has been breathed out by God," Sproul says, "He is saying that all of its ultimate origin is in him."[4]

I learned a long time ago that God's breath is more important than mine.

The Scripture we hold in our hands and ingest into our hearts and minds actually comes from *within* God. I encourage you to think about this truth throughout today. Out of the overflow of the heart the mouth speaks. When you breathe out, you're expiring what is within. So that when God breathes it out, he's breathing out to us that which has come from within him. We are reading the very heart of God—breathed out to us.

Thank him today for his indescribable gift.

- What truth is God communicating to me right now?

- How is God inviting me to respond?

Wednesday

James 1:22-25

Beautiful

Sanctify them in the truth; your word is truth.

John 17:17

I first met my wife in a church. Somebody pointed her out to me, and I'm a normal, red-blooded guy. I saw this attractive lady and said out loud, "Who's she? She's pretty."

My friends said, "She's a nurse." I fell to the floor on the spot. When that failed to attract her attention, I squinted through one open eye to tell my friend to start screaming, "He needs mouth-to-mouth!"

I'm still enamored with my wife's physical beauty, and I admit it's what initially attracted me to her. But her spiritual beauty captivated me most after I got to know her.

There is nothing wrong with physical beauty. The Bible teaches in 1 Corinthians 6:19 that our body is the temple of the Holy Spirit and we are to treat it as such. We are to care for it and present ourselves well. Yet most important is our inner beauty, the masterpiece that the Lord is shaping through a process he calls sanctification.

In the Great High Priestly Prayer of John 17, Jesus pauses on the night before his crucifixion to draw alone with his Father. His concern? Us. His children. He prayed for every believer of every age, asking God to sanctify us with his truth.

The word sanctify means to set apart, and it describes the rest-of-your-life process God undertakes to make every believer look and live more like Jesus after we are saved.

First Timothy 4:8 states that physical exercise has some value but spiritual exercise is much more important, for it promises a reward in both this life and the next. A healthy lifestyle is important, yet nothing is more crucial than disciplining ourselves in the weightier matters of God's Word and the Christian walk. Daily prayer, Bible study, and obedience are the only regimen that produces Christlikeness.

James 1:21 admonishes us to receive with meekness the implanted word, to soak in the only real truth in this world, so that it changes us from the inside out. This idea is found even in the Old Testament: "But the word is very near you. It is in your mouth and in your heart" (Deuteronomy 30:14).

If we want to radiate the purest form of beauty, we will receive God's Word, and, as James says, be a doer of the Word. It's one thing to read Scripture. It's another thing to let it search us and to apply it. When we don't follow the Holy Spirit's guidance to become doers (obeyers) of the Word, James says we're like people who go to a mirror, see what's wrong with our appearance, and do nothing about it.

And if you could ever see me staring at the mirror first thing in the morning, you'd get James' drift.

- What truth is God communicating to me right now?

- How is God inviting me to respond?

Thursday

HEBREWS 4:12

REAL FOOD

Your word is a lamp to my feet and a light to my path.
PSALM 119:105

I DON'T KNOW IF YOU'RE LIKE ME, but late at night I like to go to the refrigerator and open the door. Sometimes I just stand there and stare.

At this point, I usually begin to mutter: "We have nothing to eat in this house. Nothing."

You've probably had the same experience. We'll shut the refrigerator door and go do something, and then 30 minutes later, what do we do? We shuffle right back to the same refrigerator, open the same door, and stare at the same shelves—as if the Food Fairy came 10 minutes earlier and left something new.

Aren't you glad that when we put our faith in Christ we will never hunger or thirst spiritually again? His Word is alive. Every single time we seek him in Scripture, his Word can give us something new.

In John 6:51 Jesus says, "I am the living bread that came down from heaven. If anyone eats of this bread, he will live forever." Jesus uses another analogy in John 4:14: "But whoever drinks of the water that I will give him will never be thirsty again. The water that I will give him will become in him a spring of water welling up to eternal life."

While these verses speak primarily of salvation, the Bread of Life and the Living Water refreshes us day by day through his precious Word. He is our source of spiritual nourishment, and the only way we can be fed is if we intentionally pull up to the serving table of Scripture and dive in.

The Bread of Life and the Living Water refreshes us day by day through his precious Word.

Have you ever experienced a moment when you're reading the Bible and a particular verse jumps out at you like never before? It speaks a truth you had never understood even though you had read it perhaps dozens of times. That is when you know you're being fed by the Bread of Life and the Living Water. Jesus says his words to us are spirit and life (John 6:63). Hebrews 4:12 says that God's Word is living and active. When you crack open the Bible, you are searching out the only source of truth in a dark, dark world.

When you open this door with a hungry heart, the light always comes on, and there's always something fresh and new.

- What truth is God communicating to me right now?

- How is God inviting me to respond?

Friday

JOHN 4:10-15

HANKERING

My son, be attentive to my words; incline your ear to my sayings. For they are life to those who find them.
PROVERBS 4:20, 22

I'M WHAT MY WIFE CALLS a sneaky eater. If you've never heard of that, let me illustrate since I'm a big boy and know snack foods better than the average bear.

My wife buys these certain cakes at the grocery store bakery. They're rectangular sheet cakes with one layer and butter cream icing. Oh my! The icing alone is worth the price. When it's named after two of your favorite ingredients—butter and cream—it has to be good. But Donna confuses me. I don't know why she buys these cakes. On one hand, she eats healthy and turns up her nose at sweets. On the other chunky hand, she sees me hovering around the counter where the cake is and says, "Don't you touch that cake." Well now, is it a whatnot? Is there a small crank on the side that will play a chime? Is it a fat man's version of a flower vase?

I know the cake is sitting in the kitchen when I awake at 3 a.m. That's about the time I usually have a hankering for a piece of cake. But I don't want her to know, so I have to sneak it. But let me tell you, those plastic containers are loud when you try to open them. I have to take my blanket with me. I look like a ghost in the dim light, but it works great when I drape it over me to muffle the sound as I pry open that container in the still of the night.

Donna keeps wondering why our blanket always smells so sweet.

"Hankering" is a Southern word. It means 'longing' or 'desire.' Our flesh has strong desires. Butter Cream-frosted cake is one of them. But so are many other cravings, some that are sinful and others that are fine but should be indulged in moderation. Can you imagine how we'd live if we were so devoted to Jesus that our lives reflected a real hankering for the things of God? What do your appetites say about your spiritual condition right now?

Do you take time to dive into the rich treasures of God's Word and try to apply his truths each day? Do you spend purposeful time in prayer? Do you do what the old-timers used to call "practicing the presence of God?" It means living with the understanding that the Spirit of the living God resides inside every believer and is ever with us, urging us, encouraging us, correcting us, coaxing us to the level paths of the Lord.

Psalm 105:4 tells us to "See the Lord and his strength; seek his presence continually!"

The psalmist also writes, "As a deer pants for flowing streams, so pants my soul for you, O God. My soul thirsts for God, for the living God" (Psalm 42:1-2). Jesus calls himself our Living Water and answers our thirst here in this world and in the next: "Then the angel showed me the river of the water of life, bright as crystal, flowing from the throne of God and of the Lamb" (Revelation 22:1).

- What truth is God communicating to me right now?

- How is God inviting me to respond?

Saturday

1 Corinthians 12:12-27

Faithful One

For in one Spirit we were all baptized into one body.

1 Corinthians 12:13

My great-grandmother was the cook that Paula Deen and Martha Stewart wish they could be. I remember her glorious feasts of fried chicken that seemed like it had extra skin. She made green beans with fatback in them, and the scent reached out and yanked your taste buds through your nostrils. And she could make eggs any way you wanted them—poached, scrambled, fried, boiled…green with ham. She died at 102 years old but never counted calories, fat grams, or carbs a day in her life. She did count on you to sit your fanny at her table as long as you wanted.

Now the doctor tells me, "Eat all the eggs you want—just eat the whites of the eggs." I tried it, but it was terribly messy, and I had to go back and tell him, "But Doc, I keep cutting my mouth on that shell."

(I tell jokes for a living, so there's no such thing as a bad one.)

I remember my great-grandmother's cooking because I so fondly recall my youth. I guess you could say I grew up a little more old-fashioned. We enjoyed good Southern meals and spending quality time together. We didn't have electronic gadgets, our television got three channels, and we faithfully went to church. All the time.

Hebrews 10:25 encourages believers not to neglect meeting together. But it's not so we can check off another spiritual accomplishment. Rather, it's because God has so constructed the body of Christ that we need each other.

Paul told the church in Rome that he wanted to come visit them "that we may be mutually encouraged by each other's faith, both yours and mine" (Romans 1:12). We all have something to add, and our absence causes a void.

He knew believers would need each other to survive the travails of a world ruled by Satan.

Understanding that Jesus personally established the Church is crucial to our levying proper importance to it. He knew believers would need each other to survive the travails of a world ruled by Satan (2 Corinthians 4:4).

Church attendance across America has been on the decline for several years. Will you be a faithful one? At some point, we all must realize that it is a matter of obedience. And when we don't join in fellowship, it is to the detriment of others and our own great loss.

- What truth is God communicating to me right now?

- How is God inviting me to respond?

Sunday

GENESIS 21:8-21

DOES HE NOT HEAR?

Then God opened her eyes, and she saw a well of water.
And she went and filled the skin with water and gave the boy a drink.
GENESIS 21:19

MY WIFE SAYS I don't listen to her. The other day she cupped my chin, turned my face to look straight into my eyes, and said, "You men never hear anything. Listen!"

Then she went on and on about how I don't listen and how I always tune her out, and I think she said a few other things—I can't remember. I really wasn't paying attention. But when I snapped out of it, I realized she was right. Sometimes I don't listen intently enough at what she says. It hit me that one of the surest ways to show love and concern is to listen, and when we really love someone we can show it with our undivided attention.

This pertains to our spiritual lives as well. We can connect with God anytime, anywhere, about anything, through prayer. That is how we communicate with him. God always listens to those who are his.

Last week, we introduced the idea that God sees. He watches his children, and he knows and cares about everything that touches our lives: "For the eyes of the Lord run to and fro throughout the whole earth, to give strong support to those whose heart is blameless toward him" (2 Chronicles 16:9).

You may think, "Well, my heart is not blameless. I feel like such a loser because I blow it all the time." The message of the gospel is that you are the ultimate victor but only because of Christ. When you are covered by the blood of Jesus, your sins have been washed as white as snow. As God's child, when he looks upon you, he sees the righteousness of his Son, a righteousness that was applied to your account because of your faith in the One who died for you, was buried, and rose again.

So, yes, God sees. But the Bible also tells us that he hears.

You may remember the story of Sarah's handmaiden, Hagar, who fled from Sarah after conceiving a child with Abram. Ultimately, she returned to Sarah at God's direction. Hagar birthed Abram's first son, Ishmael. Again, it wasn't God's idea for Abram and Sarah to seek a shortcut to having a son by conceiving the child with Hagar, and the family arrangement created great strain. Another conflict arises in Genesis 21, where Sarah demands that Abram (now named Abraham) banish Hagar and Ishmael.

God allows the banishment because he has plans for Ishmael. Hagar does not know this, however. In the wilderness, as Ishmael is dying of thirst, she leaves her weakened teenage boy under a bush and walks away. As she lifts up her voice and weeps, the boy cries out too.

"And God heard the voice of the boy, and the angel of God called to Hagar from heaven and said to her, "What troubles you, Hagar? Fear not, for God has heard the voice of the boy where he is. Up! Lift up the boy, and hold him fast with your hand, for I will make him into a great nation." Then God opened her eyes, and she saw a well of water. And she went and filled the skin with water and gave the boy a drink" (Genesis 21:17-19).

The first time Hagar fled Abram and Sarah in Genesis 16, she gave the name El-Roi to her faithful God that sees. Now, as her son borders on death and cries out, she learns why God had told Abram many years earlier that her child's name would be Ishmael.

Because the word Ishmael means "God hears."

Hebrews 4:16 actually encourages us to boldly and expectantly cry out to God, to approach his throne of grace to find mercy and grace in time of need. The writer knows that we can trust God not only to hear us but also to provide his perfect answer in his perfect timing.

Here is our assurance: "And this is the confidence that we have toward him, that if we ask anything according to his will he hears us" (1 John 5:14).

The phrase "according to his will" is key. It doesn't mean we can name and claim a luxury car. It does mean that when we're walking in the light as he is in the light, when we've surrendered our will to his will, when we're obedient to his word, God will work everything for good for those who love him and are called according to his purpose. He will hear us. And he will answer.

In fact, even when we don't know exactly how to best verbalize our heart's cry, God hears—and helps us himself:

"And the Holy Spirit helps us in our weakness. For example, we don't know what God wants us to pray for. But the Holy Spirit prays for us with groanings that cannot be expressed in words" (Romans 8:26, NLT).

Through prayer, he not only hears your words but he listens to your heart.

Maybe you're in a valley right now. Maybe you're dealing with heartache or facing a challenge with no end in sight. Maybe you feel no one listens to you or even cares. Maybe it seems as if you've been placed under a prickly bush in a barren wilderness, with no hope to be found.

That's when your faith has to fill the gaps. That's when you sink your heart into 1 Peter 5:7 and cast all your cares upon Jesus, for he really does care for you. That's when you trust that the God who sees is also the God who hears.

"He who planted the ear, does he not hear? He who formed the eye, does he not see" (Psalm 94:9)?

- What truth is God communicating to me right now?

- How is God inviting me to respond?

Monday

1 THESSALONIANS 5:16-19

THE FAST LANE

Rejoice always, pray without ceasing, give thanks in all circumstances; for this is the will of God in Christ Jesus for you.

1 THESSALONIANS 5:16-18

INTERSTATE TRAFFIC IN DOWNTOWN Atlanta was thick, as usual. I worried it would make me late for a midweek speaking engagement at a church, so I hopped in the fast lane on the far left—the one that is supposed to move. It was only natural that I would get behind a lady driving a boat of a car. It was so massive you could've landed a plane on it, and it was going the minimum speed. I didn't even know interstates had minimum speeds until I suddenly was going slow enough to read the signs.

She appeared to be about 115 years old. All I saw were knuckles on the steering wheel, a big bouffant hairdo, and a left blinker indicating that she apparently planned to turn into the concrete median.

In a huff, I rolled down my window and screamed, "Move it, woman!" Instantly, I was convicted. In his sweet but firm way, the Holy Spirit reminded me, "You're an evangelist, and this is how you want to be seen? This woman may be a member of the church where you're going to speak. She may be coming to hear you."

Ouch.

Right then I prayed. I didn't lie across the dashboard of my car. I didn't shut my eyes in the fast lane of the interstate. I just prayed: "God, forgive me for getting so mad at this very slow woman."

I could've phrased it better, because obviously I was still a little too focused on the slow driver. Yet as I think back, I'm reminded of why I even reacted in prayer. Why do I think it's even plausible to try to talk to the God of the universe while stuck in a car in the middle of the road? Here's why:

"Since then we have a great high priest who has passed through the heavens, Jesus, the Son of God, let us hold fast our confession. For we do not have a high priest who is unable to sympathize with our weaknesses, but one who in every respect has been tempted as we are, yet without sin. Let us then with confidence draw near to the throne of grace, that we may receive mercy and find grace to help in time of need" (Hebrews 4:14–16).

One of the great treasures of the believer is that God himself is our sympathetic advocate. He knows our faults intimately, and he knows what it feels like to be human. It's one of the reasons God came to Earth in the form of man. Scripture also says there is one mediator between God and man, the man Christ Jesus (1 Timothy 2:5). We don't have to go through anyone else.

When 1 Thessalonians 5:17 tells us to pray without ceasing, it means to walk through each day with a heart tilted toward our Savior. It doesn't mean becoming a monk and staying on callused knees. It means living faithfully and ever ready to call out to God for any need. All day long, be prepared to have short conversations with your heavenly Father, asking for his wisdom, for his intervention for others, and for whatever you encounter.

Anytime, anywhere, in any situation you can personally talk to the Lord. This unfathomable gift is what Jesus secured for us on the Cross. He doesn't just invite us to use it. He expects it.

- What truth is God communicating to me right now?

- How is God inviting me to respond?

Tuesday

PHILIPPIANS 2:1-11

HUSBAND CHAIR

Let each of you look not only to his own interests, but also to the interests of others.
PHILIPPIANS 2:4

MOST OF US MEN would rather have our back molars pulled out without Novocain than go to the mall to look at shoes for six hours. My wife, however, lives for that moment.

I've learned a secret. Every time my wife wants me to go shopping, the first thing I look for is the Husband Chair. Many department stores have a few of these chairs scattered around the women's sections. I don't really notice them in the men's sections because men are on a mission when they shop. They don't want to sit around. But most women's sections include a pit stop for the men.

I'm pretty sure store architects have been dragged around shopping with their wives, so they design the place with one thought in mind: *Settle in, son, it's going to be a while.*

Not long ago, I was out shopping with Donna and started walking toward the Husband Chair only to find a fellow already sitting there. He pulled a gun on me and said one word.

"Taken."

I'm exaggerating about the gun, but his look threw daggers. It reminded me that we all can be our worst in times of stress. I love traveling but hate airports because few places bring out the worst in people like airports. Something about trying to get somewhere but not being in total control freaks out people.

During the few times I've played golf, I've noticed a sign on the first tee that declares the rules. It says, "The first rule of golf is consideration of others." Humans are so bad that even while playing a game that's supposed to be relaxing we still need rules on behavior.

We want to be seen as being good and righteous, and we naturally act in our own best interests.

Philippians 2:4 states, "Let each of you look not only to his own interests, but also to the interests of others." The only way anyone can ever go against fallen human nature and consistently look out for the interests of others is through the power of the Holy Spirit.

The great Puritan preacher Jonathan Edwards dissected human nature enough to observe that even our virtuous actions stem from pride or fear—pride because it makes us feel superior to others or fear because we don't want to lose out or be punished by God. We want to be seen as being good and righteous, and we naturally act in our own best interests. So, even at his best, fallen man is sinful.

Only the revolutionary gospel of Jesus Christ permeating our hearts can change us to esteem others better than ourselves (Philippians 2:3).

Many times my wife and I accompany each other just for the sake of being together. I don't like to shop as much and she does, but I like her company, so I consider her interests over mine. Besides, I know a Husband Chair is waiting. (See, Jonathan Edwards was right.)

- What truth is God communicating to me right now?

- How is God inviting me to respond?

Wednesday

Luke 5:17-26

The Greatest Need

For I am not ashamed of the gospel, for it is the power of God for salvation to everyone who believes.

Romans 1:16

I'M A FOOD ADDICT who also happens to have a bad back. I'm embarrassed to say that when I weighed more than 300 pounds my back went out on me, and I couldn't move off of the couch to get to the bathroom. I had to call 911.

The paramedics who came were women. Little women.

The ladies walked in and stopped in their tracks when they saw this massive beached whale with a locked-up back and full bladder.

"Oh my," one of them said before she knew it. The other paramedic leaned toward her partner and whispered without turning her face.

"We might need some backup."

I wanted to crawl under a cushion. I've heard of police needing backup, but paramedics?

My dainty helpers dispensed with the required blood pressure and heart rate checks, asked me a few questions, and radioed the situation back to headquarters. They didn't exactly have a walkie-talkie code for "lard-butt needs a lift," so they just said it—in a professional manner, of course.

"Um, yes, um, we're on location. Subject is incapacitated and is more than we can handle."

The radio squawked. "What's the problem?"

"We need more manpower, sir."

"More manpower? What do you mean?"

"Sir, we need assistance to lift him. He's a large individual."

"Can he not shift onto the gurney?"

"No, sir. He's incapacitated with back pain. We gotta have some muscle here."

Pause.

The greatest need any person in your life has is to know Jesus.

"Listen, we're, uh, we're really busy…are you sure you can't move him?"

She was nodding before she pressed the button. "Positive."

Pause.

"10-4. Assistance on the way."

Right about then I would've signed Dr. Kevorkian's assisted suicide release if he wanted to help send me on to Jesus.

As pitiful as this story is, it reminds me of the story in today's reading passage. It's easy to read Luke's factual account of Jesus healing the paralytic and hail as heroes the small group of men who worked to tear back the roof and lower him through the crowd to Jesus. Their actions were admirable, yes, but the truth is that they just did what friends are supposed to do for a friend in need: They took him to Jesus.

The greatest need any person in your life has is to know Jesus. As the world seemingly spins more out of control by the day, we believers remember Jesus' words in Matthew 24. So many of the devastating world events we increasingly see in the news are the very birth pangs Jesus described in signaling his imminent return. They will grow in frequency and severity.

The only answer for this lost world is Jesus. We have that answer. Think about the people in your life who need the Savior you know. Time is growing shorter by the day. Are you willing to tear back the roof?

- What truth is God communicating to me right now?

- How is God inviting me to respond?

Thursday

2 Corinthians 5:16-21

Ambassadors

All this is from God, who through Christ reconciled us to himself and gave us the ministry of reconciliation.

2 Corinthians 5:18

When I go to the mall once a year—the day after Thanksgiving—I'm like everybody else: agitated and frustrated. And that's before I park the car.

You cannot find a place to park at the mall on Black Friday. So I turn it into a game. I drive around the lot again and again until a front parking spot opens up, and I whip into this primo space. And then I sit there for an hour—with my backup lights on.

Yes, I am that guy.

I'm kidding, of course. I actually use my trips to the mall to people-watch and make new acquaintances. It's amazing what you can learn about someone just by being friendly enough to open a conversation. It's also amazing how the Lord can use that conversation to minister to hurting or lost people.

It is especially important to show love and compassion to people who don't know the Lord: "Walk in wisdom toward outsiders, making the best use of the time. Let your speech always be gracious, seasoned with salt, so that you may know how you ought to answer each person" (Colossians 4:5–6).

I'm always encouraged to watch the man-on-the-street videos produced by Way of the Master, a ministry of Ray Comfort (wayofthemaster.com). Ray is accomplished in the Scriptures and is gifted at using simple apologetic techniques to make people think about their spiritual condition. He knows all the facts and never wavers from the truth, but he disarms people with his gentle and sincere approach. He actually loves on them with the truth. In one video, he says, "All I'm doing is reasoning with you. I don't want to win an argument."[5]

It is especially important to show love and compassion to people who don't know the Lord.

All believers must remember that the Bible calls us "ambassadors for Christ" in 2 Corinthians 5:20. We have to ask ourselves why God chose to leave us on Earth after saving us. Why didn't he just take us on home after we surrendered our hearts to him?

It was for one reason. One thing we can do on Earth that we cannot do in heaven is tell a lost person about Jesus.

"All this is from God, who through Christ reconciled us to himself and gave us the ministry of reconciliation; that is, in Christ God was reconciling the world to himself, not counting their trespasses against them, and entrusting to us the message of reconciliation" (2 Corinthians 5:18–19).

God has entrusted to us this greatest of treasures. What will you do with it today?

- What truth is God communicating to me right now?

- How is God inviting me to respond?

Friday

1 Peter 3:14-17

We All Have A Story

Declare his glory among the nations, his marvelous works among all the peoples!

Psalm 96:3

Saul of Tarsus was a devout orthodox Jew who studied at the feet of one of Israel's leading scholars, Gamaliel, and earned a seat on the elite religious ruling council called the Sanhedrin.

Saul persecuted Christians, which he and his contemporaries considered a cult called The Way. He helped preside over the stoning murder of Stephen. He dragged Christians to prison and was headed all the way to Damascus to arrest more followers of The Way when Jesus appeared to him. Acts 9 records the miraculous encounter that led to Saul of Tarsus becoming the Apostle Paul, the greatest Christian evangelist in world history. The remainder of Acts records no fewer than 10 sermons Paul preaches to everyone from Jewish Synagogue leaders to the Jerusalem Temple elite to high-brow Greek philosophers to Roman governors to the king of Israel to, finally, Jewish leaders in Rome. There, he was beheaded by sword a little more than three decades after Christ's crucifixion.

We all have a story. Yours may not be as dramatic and fantastic as Paul's, and your audience may not be as esteemed as Paul's, but your salvation is just as much a miracle as Paul's. If you're a Christian, then you have a personal testimony, and there's power in your story. The challenge lies in finding the courage to share it.

I once met a doctor who used his practice to share the gospel. He had a captive audience, and he treated their physical ailments before doctoring their spiritual one. After I met him, a friend asked me, "Did the doctor witness to you?"

If you're a Christian, then you have a personal testimony, and there's power in your story.

"No," I said. "I guess he already knew I was a Christian because under 'Occupation' on the paperwork I wrote, 'Minister.'"

"Last year, this guy won more than two hundred people to Jesus in his doctor's office," he said. "One on one, just telling them about Jesus."

I did confirm that the doctor didn't stand there with a Bible in one hand and needle in the other and say, "If you died today, do you know where you'd go?"

He didn't do that. He just let Jesus' love flow through him.

You don't have to be a theologian to share your story. You can be a witness for Christ by sharing your story and walking someone through John 3:16. It's that simple. You already have that verse memorized.

People can try to dispute the Bible, but one thing they cannot disclaim is your story: "I was this person before Jesus.

I'm this person now because of Jesus." No one can disprove the difference in a true believer transformed by Jesus.

"Those who are wise shall shine like the brightness of the sky above; and those who turn many to righteousness, like the stars forever and ever" (Daniel 12:3).

- What truth is God communicating to me right now?

- How is God inviting me to respond?

Saturday

JAMES 2:14-26

WHATEVER OUR HANDS FIND TO DO

So also faith by itself, if it does not have works, is dead.

JAMES 2:17

I'M A SLOW LEARNER. Just ask my wife. We've been married two decades, and she still has to train me on exactly how a house is supposed to be kept. I haven't achieved the Donna Housekeeping Seal of Approval, but I'm learning.

She told me recently she wanted me to vacuum the rug. I shook my head in protest.

"Listen, I do the lawn. It looks pristine. I ride on my mower and make it look perfect," I said. "Now, when they come out with a riding vacuum cleaner, I'm all in."

After a quick scowl, she harped on me about making up the bed.

"Make up the bed?" I asked. "Why do we have to make up the bed when we're going to get right back in it in four hours?"

My wife says I sometimes revert back to the arguments of a 10-year-old in my reasoning. While she may have a point, the Bible addresses our work habits. Some people are naturally driven to complete projects, while others are apathetic and need motivation to get moving. Me? I'm inclined to work very hard if it comes with a Dairy Queen Blizzard.

Laziness, which is a lifestyle for some, is a temptation for all of us. The Bible only reaches 15 verses into its second chapter when God ordains work for man: "The Lord God took the man and put him in the garden of Eden to work it and keep it" (Genesis 2:15). Since God expects man to work, we inherently know laziness is a sin.

God created man to work for a reason, because whatever our hands find to do, we are to do it with all our might.

Still, the Lord is serious enough about the subject that he pointedly addresses laziness in Proverbs 6:6-11: "Go to the ant, O sluggard; consider her ways, and be wise. Without having any chief, officer, or ruler, she prepares her bread in summer and gathers her food in harvest. How long will you lie there, O sluggard? When will you arise from your sleep? A little sleep, a little slumber, a little folding of the hands to rest, and poverty will come upon you like a robber, and want like an armed man."

I love the New Living Translation's frank interpretation of Verse 6: "Take a lesson from the ants, you lazybones."

Proverbs 26:14 provides another strong image: "As a door turns on its hinges, so does a sluggard on his bed."

God created man to work for a reason, because whatever our hands find to do, we are to do it with all of our might (Ecclesiastes 9:10). When we obey God's Word by working hard at whatever he has tasked us to do in life, it is an act of worship. Ephesians 2:10 states, "For we are his workmanship, created in Christ Jesus for good works, which God prepared beforehand, that we should walk in them."

We are not saved by works, but we show our faith by our works. Today, determine to work heartily for the Lord and not for man. Take the attitude of a servant devoted to your Lord, and see what a difference it makes.

- What truth is God communicating to me right now?

- How is God inviting me to respond?

Week Five

Sunday

James 1:12-15

For Freedom

Blessed is the man who remains steadfast under trial, for when he has stood the test he will receive the crown of life ...

James 1:12

I love everything about food. I love the way it looks. I love the way it glistens in the light. I love the steam that comes off of it. The box it comes in. The table it goes on. The trash-can it goes in afterward. I love just saying the word *food.*

Some people are addicted to crack cocaine. Some people are addicted to weed. Others are addicted to gambling. Me? I'm addicted to Krispy Kreme donuts.

I understand addictive personalities. We all struggle with something. My struggle happens to be with food. I cannot tell you how many times I have failed and felt shame for my lack of discipline and self-control. Despite knowing all of the health hazards of being overweight, despite being chastised, coaxed, and cajoled by relatives, friends, and doctors, I have spent most of my adult life returning over and over to the same struggle.

I praise the Lord that today I manage my eating habits better than I did in the past, but it's still a battle I wage every day.

Perhaps you don't struggle with overeating, but you likely battle some habit you wish were not in your life. All of us grapple with the flesh; our desires may not match, but the source of those desires is the same. Today's reading passage in James highlights that source. We can say the devil made us do it, but the truth is we like to sin. We are lured and enticed by our own desires that well up from our flesh and manifest themselves in the particular appetites that drive each of us.

The antidote is found at the beginning of two Chapter 12s.

Romans 12:2 states: "Do not be conformed to this world, but be transformed by the renewal of your mind." And the only way to renew your mind is through consistency in prayer and study of God's Word—and obedience to it.

Then we should remember Hebrews 12:1-2. "Therefore, since we are surrounded by so great a cloud of witnesses, let us also lay aside every weight, and sin which clings so closely, and let us run with endurance the race that is set before us, looking to Jesus, the founder and perfecter of our faith, who for the joy that was set before him endured the cross, despising the shame, and is seated at the right hand of the throne of God."

Maybe you've messed up and done something you should not have done. Maybe it was the same thing you've done seemingly a thousand times. Remember, Jesus is the way, the truth, and the life who endured the cross and despised the shame he went through on our behalf. He not only took our deserved punishment, but he also took our shame.

He is the way of escape. He is the truth of the matter. He is the life you seek.

Every Man's Battle by Stephen Arterburn and Fred Stoeker is a powerful study on the common struggle with lust suffered by most men. Perhaps the most effective tool the authors provide is for believers to honor James 5:16 and confess our sins to one another. The only way sin survives and grows is in the dark. When we bring sin to the light, it is much easier to kill.

He is the way of escape. He is the truth of the matter. He is the life you seek.

"Take no part in the unfruitful works of darkness, but instead expose them. For it is shameful even to speak of the things that they do in secret. But when anything is exposed by the light, it becomes visible, for anything that becomes visible is light. Therefore it says, 'Awake, O sleeper, and arise from the dead, and Christ will shine on you'" (Ephesians 5:14).

The prophet Jeremiah relays that God's eyes are on all of our ways and sin is not concealed from his eyes (Jeremiah 16:17). So we're not fooling the most important Person. If we're not fooling the most important Person, it only makes sense to be real with fellow believers who also grapple with desires that drive them to err.

Find a Christian friend or two whom you know you can trust to be confidential. Share with them your struggle. Ask them for prayer and counsel. Meet with them regularly if needed. One of the real breakdowns in the Church today is that believers don't seek help from each other as God intended. It is incredibly freeing to admit your failures to someone who understands and loves you.

It was for freedom that Christ set us free from our fallen state of sin. (Galatians 5:1) Say that to yourself. It was for freedom that Christ set us free. Stand firm therefore, and do not submit again to a yoke of slavery to sin. Throw yourself on Christ today. Truly yield all you have and all you are to him and taste the freedom he offers.

- What truth is God communicating to me right now?

- How is God inviting me to respond?

Monday

MATTHEW 16:13-20

CHOICES

And on this rock I will build my church, and the gates of hell shall not prevail against it.

MATTHEW 16:18

WE WERE IN DES MOINES, IOWA for a show at a church when my wife fell and twisted her ankle so badly that she couldn't walk. When we reached the hotel, they had no wheelchair, so I fetched the portable luggage rack.

"Honey, hop on here," I said, and rolled her right through the lobby. You should've seen the look she gave me when I told the bellhop I didn't need help with my old bag.

The next morning we had to fly back home to Atlanta, and her ankle was no better when we reached the airport security line. She couldn't use the scanners because she was in a wheelchair, so they had to pat her down. It seemed like the TSA lady spent extra time on the search because it was an unusual situation. I looked at the agent and said, "Ma'am, I'm married to her and can't touch her that much!"

Donna cut her eyes at me again.

All of this was to get on a 6 a.m. flight to make it home in time for our small group at church. We try to do that because we value that time with fellow believers. We think it's important because they're our family. If you know Jesus as your Savior, we're all family, and we should devote ourselves to assembling together in worship of our Lord and in fellowship with each other.

Jesus personally established the church for a reason. He desired corporate worship here on earth (corporate worship will be eternal in heaven!), and he knew believers would need to love and support each other as they grow in his Word in an increasingly hostile world.

While it is true that a person can find fellowship in a bar or club, he or she still will walk out the door empty. When a body of spirit-filled believers share community, it fosters relationships that fulfill us through spiritual growth in this life and also bear eternal gravity.

The movie *Shawshank Redemption* features several poignant moments, none more full of gravity than when lead characters Andy Dufresne and "Red" Redding sit in the prison courtyard with their backs against the cold block walls late in the movie. A resolute Andy has just emerged from a long turn in solitary confinement, and he does little more than stare and speak in monotone through one last conversation with his buddy before escaping Shawshank prison. Red knows something is wrong. He protests Andy's desperate talk but can only listen as Andy spits out a line that still resonates with me.

"Comes down to a simple choice, really," Andy says. "Get busy livin' or get busy dyin."

The sobering truth is that every day we either get busy

living or get busy dying. Our choices make or break us. People make time to do what they really want to do. Where on the scale of living or dying is your devotion to the Lord? To your church?

- What truth is God communicating to me right now?

- How is God inviting me to respond?

Tuesday

LUKE 6:43-45

OH HUSH

For out of the abundance of the heart his mouth speaks.

LUKE 6:45

I WANT TO SHARE a little truth with you. Men can be—let's see, how should I say this?—insensitive.

I'll admit it. It's true. Men can make the most mindless comments imaginable, and then five seconds later we don't remember what we said. But ladies never forget. Sometimes it takes months before ladies make sure to remind us what we said, but one universal truth remains.

Ladies. Never. Forget.

I remember taking a girlfriend on a date in college. As I drove along with the young lady in the passenger seat, I said something she didn't like. I didn't think anything of it at that moment and still don't remember what I said, but she didn't say a word for miles. All I saw was the back of her head as she glared out of her window.

Eventually, I worked up the nerve to break the silence.

"What's the matter?" I asked.

Not a word.

"Honey, what's wrong?"

Not a word.

"C'mon, tell me what's going on?"

She whipped around and in a guttural voice that sounded like something out of *The Exorcist* exclaimed, "Nothing, leave me alone." I expected her head to start spinning and green stuff to start spewing out.

The problem must be with me though. For the first two years of my marriage to Donna, I thought my name was, "Oh Hush."

If there's a commonality among all people of every culture, it's the misuse of the tongue. James, the half-brother of Jesus, addressed this constant weakness.

"The tongue is a small member, yet it boasts of great things. How great a forest is set ablaze by such a small fire! And the tongue is a fire, a world of unrighteousness. The tongue is set among our members, staining the whole body, setting on fire the entire course of life, and set on fire by hell" (James 3:5-6).

If we think back over the times we've gotten ourselves into trouble, invariably our mouths led the way. Why? Because the mouth is only an instrument, an outlet, for what is in our hearts (Luke 6:45). We can learn from our past mistakes and muzzle future ones by following God's Proverbs prescriptions:

"Whoever guards his mouth preserves his life; he who opens wide his lips comes to ruin" (13:3).

"The beginning of strife is like letting out water, so quit before the quarrel breaks out" (17:14).

"A fool's lips walk into a fight, and his mouth invites a beating" (18:6).

"Whoever keeps his mouth and his tongue keeps himself out of trouble" (21:23).

Our words mean something. They can be used for great good or great evil. And, as all of us have learned the hard way, they can't be taken back once they are spoken. Today, let's begin the hard work of thinking and measuring before speaking.

- What truth is God communicating to me right now?

- How is God inviting me to respond?

Wednesday

MATTHEW 7:1-5

THE LORD LOOKS ON THE HEART

Do not judge according to appearance, but judge with righteous judgment.

JOHN 7:24 (NKJV)

THE OTHER DAY AT WAL-MART I saw a woman—not a girl, not a teenager, not a young child, but a full-grown woman—shopping in her pajama bottoms. She sported fuzzy slippers and plaid flannel PJs right there for all the world to see.

Perhaps you've seen someone do this in public before. I don't know—I might have seen you do it. But I watched her shop in her pajamas and was taken aback with one thought:

"Wow…that's not a bad idea!"

A few days later, Donna was missing one final ingredient for a meal she was cooking. She hurried me to the grocery store, but just as I walked out the door I heard, "No!"

She caught me trying to sneak out in my pajama bottoms.

"Put some pants on!" she said.

"Why? I'm just running to the grocery store for two minutes."

"Not in this neighborhood," she said. "People know me."

You've heard the old saying, "Don't judge a book by its cover." Well, that can be true in this case too. I'm not advocating that we all run to town in our pajamas—and I'm certain my Baptist daddy would insist on putting on our best in public for the Lord. But we should be careful about making assumptions as well. What if the lady I saw in Wal-Mart had been up all night with a sick baby? What if she was undergoing chemo and was exerting every ounce of energy she had to buy a few groceries? Or maybe she was just doing her best and her best happened to be pajamas at that moment. No matter what, Jesus loves that pajama-wearing Wal-Mart lady. When we look at people, that's what we should see first: a person loved by Jesus.

First Samuel 16 records the prophet Samuel's anointing of David as the next king of Israel. God's selection of David was stunning, especially in contrast to his much older and more accomplished brothers. David didn't measure up at all, and even Samuel was puzzled. But then Samuel learned this lesson: "For the Lord sees not as man sees: man looks on the outward appearance, but the Lord looks on the heart" (v. 7).

We never fully know other people's hearts or circumstances. It's easy to judge and categorize, but in every single case we don't know all the facts. We should always use godly discernment, but we should also live in godly grace.

Maybe the next time we're tempted to size up people, we should just pray for God's mercy and grace upon them and love them like Jesus. Maybe we should remember that the Lord indeed looks on the heart, and that includes ours.

- What truth is God communicating to me right now?

- How is God inviting me to respond?

Thursday

EPHESIANS 4:17-27

SMART CAR

Put on the new self, created after the likeness of God in true righteousness and holiness.

EPHESIANS 4:24

WHEN I WAS MUCH HEAVIER several years ago, I traveled to Chicago. I'm cheap, so I rented the cheapest car I could find. I looked at the price, not the type of car. When I got to the counter, I found out that I had rented a subcompact economy car.

The clerk offered me the keys and a smile: "Mr. Davis, your car is in Space A-12."

I walked out to the parking lot and headed toward A12 when I immediately spotted the car. I thought, "Hmmm. My perspective must be a little off. It must just look small because it's so far across the parking lot." Then I walked three feet and bumped into it.

I found an attendant who told me it was called a Smart Car. It was so small that I thought it had broken off of a normal car. It looked like a Tic-Tac. Or a Skittle. I didn't know whether to drive it or eat it.

It made me realize that I'd best behave while driving. If I got into road rage with anyone, all they'd have to do is roll down their window and push my car into the ditch.

When I get behind the wheel, it helps to remember that Ephesians 4:26 tells us to "Be angry and do not sin; do not let the sun go down on your anger."

It's a good discipline to memorize Scripture, to absorb it and allow the Holy Spirit to transform your mind by implanting God's Word into you. God's Word is a purifying agent, and Ephesians 5:25-26 says Christ cleanses his body of believers "by the washing of water with the word." Further, Jesus himself promises us that his Holy Spirit will bring his Word to our remembrance when we need it…

It's a good discipline to memorize Scripture, to absorb it and allow the Holy Spirit to transform your mind by implanting God's Word into you.

Like when we're on the road. Or in a tense moment with our spouse. Or when we disagree with a co-worker or fellow student.

"Know this, my beloved brothers: let every person be quick to hear, slow to speak, slow to anger; for the anger of man does not produce the righteousness of God. Therefore put away all filthiness and rampant wickedness and receive with meekness the implanted word, which is able to save your souls" (James 1:19–21).

God indeed implants his Word in our hearts and through his Holy Spirit gives us recall of his truths. If you're anything like me, especially when you're 300 pounds and driving a Tic-Tac, you need it.

- What truth is God communicating to me right now?

- How is God inviting me to respond?

Friday

PHILIPPIANS 4:8-9

A DOG'S EARS

If there is any excellence, if there is anything worthy of praise, think about these things.

PHILIPPIANS 4:8

MY NIECE, ASHLEY, WORKED in my home office for several years, helping me book my concerts and coordinate various ministries. I had one ironclad rule for her.

"If anyone calls before 10 a.m. and wonders where I am," I said, "Just tell them I'm in the word."

It took her several months to figure out I wasn't somewhere studying the Bible. I had nicknamed my bed "the word."

I was able to tell the truth, appear devout, and still be lazy all at the same time. See how devious I am? I'm halfway joking, of course, but the truth is that we all care about what other people think of us, and sometimes we'll bend the truth to make ourselves look better. We don't want to be grist for other people's rumor mill.

I love the vivid imagery of Proverbs 26:17, which warns against meddling in other people's affairs. Here is my paraphrase: "Whoever sticks his nose in someone else's business is like a dummy who is willing to grab a passing pit bull by the ears."

None of us would dare grab a strange dog by the ears. Yet

Scripture says it is just as certain that we'll get bitten by engaging in gossip, slander, assumptions, and meddling. Now you know why curiosity killed the cat. The dog ate it.

Today's reading passage encourages us to think the best of other people. In case you're not aware of how serious the Lord considers this matter, let me share three New Testament passages:

• "Aspire to live quietly, and to mind your own affairs" (1 Thessalonians 4:11).

• "For we hear that some among you walk in idleness, not busy at work, but busybodies. Now such persons we command and encourage in the Lord Jesus Christ to do their work quietly and to earn their own living" (2 Thessalonians 3:11–12).

Let us be a people who speak life rather than death.

• "If you are insulted for the name of Christ, you are blessed, because the Spirit of glory and of God rests upon you. But let none of you suffer as a murderer or a thief or an evildoer or as a meddler" (1 Peter 4:14-15).

Peter appears to be arguing from the greatest sin to the least, so he says God doesn't want us being known as either a murderer or a meddler. "Death and life are in the power of the tongue, and those who love it will eat its fruits" (Proverbs 18:21). Let us be a people who speak life rather than death.

- What truth is God communicating to me right now?

- How is God inviting me to respond?

Saturday

JOHN 1:14-17

GRACE UPON GRACE

For the law was given through Moses; grace and truth came through Jesus Christ.

JOHN 1:17

IN THE EARLY DAYS OF MY CAREER, I liked to stay with the parents of my friend Mark Lowry whenever I traveled through Virginia.

On one visit, I stayed in their basement apartment for guests. It had a large bedroom with a King-sized guest bed and a King-sized guest bathroom with a King-sized guest shower and King-sized sink. And a King-sized toilet with a King-sized oak toilet seat. A very comfortable and contoured oak toilet seat.

Did I mention that it was made of oak wood?

Now, in my defense, it was already cracked a little bit.

I was grossly overweight at the time, and when I sat on that thing it snapped. The sound reached my brain a split second before the searing pain did. It was something akin to a hornet sting in a very bad place.

I yelped like a coonhound.

When that seat snapped underneath my weight, the cracked seat pinched me and left an indelible mark way too close to the crack of my seat. It's not easy to dance when your pants are around your ankles. I managed to keep my balance as I flailed and rubbed.

I shined my bottom toward the mirror to check whether I had a gaping wound. Gaping, yes. Wound, no. I had only a small red mark surrounding a rising white welt.

What could I do—act like it didn't happen? Broken hardware was involved, and duct tape would've been too obvious. So I did what any good comedian would do. I grabbed the broken half of the seat and waddled upstairs.

"Mr. Lowry!" I yelled as I held up the seat. "Umm. Your seat broke." He looked up from his breakfast and laughed.

At the time, I was mortified. Looking back now, I giggle to myself. It's funny how growing in God's grace over time has a way of lessening the pain of our mistakes. It is the beauty of John 1:16: "For from his fullness we have all received, grace upon grace."

Christ heaps his grace upon us, pressed down and running over.

Christ heaps his grace upon us, pressed down and running over. It covers our past, holds our present, and promises our future.

I love the advice from Scottish missionary Oswald Chambers: "Let the past sleep, but let it sleep in the sweet embrace of Christ, and let us go on into the invincible future with him."[6]

- What truth is God communicating to me right now?

- How is God inviting me to respond?

Sunday

Romans 7:14-25

Filled with the Spirit

Wretched man that I am! Who will deliver me from this body of death?

Romans 7:24

My wife and I dated for years before marrying in our mid-30s. When we dated, I drove wherever we went and she sat in the passenger seat. We never had any problems with the arrangement. Now that we've been married a while, it's different.

The transformation started so slowly that at first I thought something was wrong with my car. I figured all the squeaking came from my worn engine belts. I'd hear, "Oooh, ooh, woooh, woooh, woooh." It sounded like a panicked monkey.

The noise grew louder until I finally noticed Donna holding up her hands in front of the windshield, eyes wide open.

"What is wrong with you?" I asked.

She couldn't hold it any longer. She yelled a new warning every few moments: "Look out! Red light! Watch it! Look out for that car! You're too close to their bumper! Slow down!"

"What are you doing?" I yelled. "You're going to make me wreck!"

"I'm going to make you wreck?" she said. "You've already made me a wreck."

She didn't stop. At every curve or traffic light, Donna squeaked or yelled and stomped on her imaginary break pedal to no avail. She had no control of the car. I was the one at the wheel, no matter how much she sounded like a chimp.

When we reached the interstate, she complained I manipulated the accelerator too much, up and down, up and down, rocking her back and forth.

I shook my head. "It's on cruise control, for goodness sake."

Now if you come to our small town and see us in the car, Donna is at the wheel and I'm in the passenger seat mumbling and looking like a dork.

My driving escapades picture the Christian life. When we surrender our hearts to Christ, we are reborn spiritually. But we are still human. We're not going to be perfect until we get to heaven, and we're going to face the same temptations we've always faced. But it's different now because we are different. We now have the power not to cave in to those temptations even when we hear the devil barking in our ears.

Not that I'm calling my wife the devil, but you know what I'm saying.

The more we allow the Holy Spirit to drive our lives, Satan can chirp all he wants but he doesn't have control anymore.

It may seem odd, but, to me, one of the most inspiring passages in the Bible is today's Scripture reading in Romans.

The Apostle Paul models transparency for every believer. He admits that the things he does not want to do are the very things he winds up doing while failing to do the things he really wants to do. It's a universal fault in all of us. It goes to show that as long as we are wrapped in our flesh we will battle its carnal desires—no matter how "spiritual" we are. It's the curse of our fallen sin nature.

At least Paul also provides help to overcome this dilemma. In Ephesians 5:18, he tells us to be "filled with the Spirit." We all know that the Holy Spirit indwells us at salvation, but what does it mean to be filled with the Spirit?

God chose us and saved us. We are his.

I love Pastor John Piper's simple definition. He says it means having great joy in God.[7] Paul himself backs up this idea. He follows his admonition to be filled with the Spirit by telling us to address "one another in psalms and hymns and spiritual songs, singing and making melody to the Lord with your heart, giving thanks always and for everything to God the Father in the name of our Lord Jesus Christ" (Ephesians 5:19–20).

This doesn't mean we sing to each other all the time. It just means that believers should live with a joyous and grateful spirit of obedience and submission to the Lord, making life a faith-filled adventure.

In other words, our entire existence on Earth should be consciously predicated on the very same reason we will be joyous in eternity: God chose us and saved us. We are his.

Rejoicing in that revelation fills you with the Spirit.

Romans 15:13 states: "May the God of hope fill you with all joy and peace in believing, so that by the power of the Holy Spirit you may abound in hope." We first believe God and believe in God (and even that belief is the gift of God), and then through the power of the Holy Spirit (being filled with the Spirit) we abound in hope.

Read how Paul describes those precious ones who belong to Jesus. Meditate on this beauty: "But our citizenship is in heaven. And we eagerly await a Savior from there, the Lord Jesus Christ, who, by the power that enables Him to bring everything under his *control*, will transform our lowly bodies so that they will be like his glorious body" (Philippians 3:20-21, emphasis mine).

We're already citizens of heaven. When we live in celebration of this reality, we will finally do what we really want to do and cease doing what we don't want to do. And we will experience what it means to be filled with the Spirit.

- What truth is God communicating to me right now?

- How is God inviting me to respond?

Monday

JOHN 10:1-11

ABUNDANT LIFE

When he has brought out all his own, he goes before them, and the sheep follow him, for they know his voice.

JOHN 10:4

MY WIFE TRAVELS TO MY SHOWS with me, which gives us plenty of time to get to know each other better, sometimes too well. She constantly says I'm cheap and tacky.

I don't think I'm either. I think I'm frugal and practical. I upset her the other day when I bought her a bag of generic Cheese Puffs—the kind that come in a plain white bag with big black letters: CHEESE PUFFS. She really got mad when she read the fine print at the bottom of the bag: "Or can be used as packing material."

Hey, the Party Size bag was $4.99 per case. We had enough packing material to move to Montana with our teeth caked in orange the whole way.

Donna reminds me that God isn't cheap, and she's right. The life he promised us is full and abundant and eternal. Jesus says that the enemy comes to steal, kill, and destroy, and the results of his work are evident in the evil world system he controls. Satan cannot have the believer's soul, but unless we are on guard and walking with Jesus, the enemy certainly can neutralize our effectiveness for Christ's kingdom. He can steal our joy, kill our dreams, and destroy our homes.

But Jesus came to give us abundant life. Be careful not to equate this with material wealth or status. Jesus knows our real needs and promises to take care of them (Matthew 6:25-34). Unfortunately, the peddlers of the Prosperity Gospel have hijacked passages like these to claim they mean God is ready for his bottle to be rubbed at our every whim so he will grant us our wishes.

Abundant life means eternal life. We often think of eternal life in terms of quantity, meaning we're going to live forever after we physically die. This is true, but it's only part of the picture. Eternal life has already begun for the believer. It includes the here and now, and Jesus says he came to give you abundant life in your eternity. He's speaking about an immeasurable upgrade not only in quantity but also in quality.

The ESV Study Bible gives this definition: "Jesus calls his followers, not to a dour, lifeless, miserable existence that squashes human potential, but to a rich, full, joyful life, one overflowing with meaningful activities under the personal favor and blessing of God and in continual fellowship with his people."[8]

It doesn't mean you'll get a Mercedes. It means you already have something of infinitely more worth. You have Christ, the hope of glory.

- What truth is God communicating to me right now?

- How is God inviting me to respond?

Tuesday

MATTHEW 6:19-21

THANK GOD

"Therefore do not worry about tomorrow, for tomorrow will worry about its own things."
MATTHEW 6:34 (NKJV)

DON'T EVER BUY A CAR named after an insect—Beetle, Bug, Hornet, whatever. I bought a Dodge Maggot once. It'd go from zero to 150 degrees in 10 seconds. But even the worst clunker I ever owned was still something for which I was thankful. It got me from Point A to Point B, most of the time, safely, and I'm not sure what I would've done without it.

One thing I learned from my parents is that either your circumstances can shape your attitude, or your attitude can shape your circumstances. It's more biblical to choose the latter.

Even when we don't have the best of things, we should make the best of what we have and be thankful. The best of things for the believer are yet to come. We will never fully realize the best of things on this Earth, which is why Jesus himself tells us to lay up our treasures in heaven. Where our treasures are, our hearts are sure to follow.

Our investments, then, should be focused on eternal returns. When we do justly, love mercy, and walk humbly before our God; when we walk in his will by loving him and serving others in his name, we place our treasures in heaven (Micah 6:8). The more we send ahead of us, the more our hearts are focused on where our treasures lie.

Being thankful isn't just something we should do before we scarf down turkey on a Thursday in November. Being thankful should be the permanent inclination of our hearts. The Apostle James was Jesus' half-brother. He writes: "Count it all joy, my brothers, when you meet trials of various kinds, for you know that the testing of your faith produces steadfastness" (James 1:2-3). It's counterintuitive to our flesh to conceive of being thankful for trials. But James reminds us that we can recount God's blessings even in the worst of circumstances and realize that, just as he brought us through past tribulations, he will bring good out of our current circumstances.

First Thessalonians 5:18 leaves no wiggle room: "Be thankful in all circumstances, for this is the will of God in Christ Jesus for you." It means both your thankfulness and your current circumstances are God's will for you—so be grateful for how the Lord is working. When we find ourselves overwhelmed with burdens and worries about tomorrow, we can praise God for who he is and his promise to never leave us or forsake us.

- What truth is God communicating to me right now?

- How is God inviting me to respond?

Wednesday

EPHESIANS 4:25-32

PURSUE PEACE

Be kind to one another, tenderhearted, forgiving one another, as God in Christ forgave you.

EPHESIANS 4:32

I LIKE TO HAVE A BOWL of cereal at night. Maybe you can relate. Sometimes it's two bowls, but I do like my nighttime cereal. I pour my large bowl of cereal, I sit in my favorite chair, and I put my feet up on the coffee table and watch my TV show. And that's how I eat my bowl of cereal.

I usually ignore my wife cutting her eyes over at me.

When I'm done with my cereal, I take my feet off the coffee table, set the bowl right there on the coffee table, and put my feet back up.

I usually ignore my wife's sighs.

Because, apparently, you're not supposed to do that. Never mind putting up my feet on the table. No, I've learned that supposedly it's a Defcon 5 national security breach to leave out a cereal bowl without immediately rinsing it. If you leave out a cereal bowl, it will get all dried out and crusty and hard to wash. You have to go rinse it out. Or so I hear. Apparently you're not supposed to let the dog lick it, either. Bless his heart, he sits on his haunches and stares at that glistening bowl for 20 minutes. At least let him lick the thing, right?

You can tell that I've gotten into trouble doing this before. As I think about getting along with Donna, I realize that there's really nothing wrong with my leaving my cereal bowl on the table when I'm done. It's not like I'm sinning. But if I want peace in my home, I better show some consideration for my wife's preferences.

Romans 14:19 says, "So then let us pursue what makes for peace and for mutual upbuilding." Romans 12:18 is even more direct: "If possible, so far as it depends on you, live peaceably with all." Meditate on that for a moment. To the degree that it is in our personal power, God says to live at peace with everyone. This instruction not only covers a bowl with milk residue, but it covers all aspects of marriage, work relationships, and race relations. There is no room for hard feelings in a heart washed with the blood of Jesus.

There is no room for hard feelings in a heart washed with the blood of Jesus.

So far as it depends on you…

Love everyone, regardless of the past. Seek peace, regardless of the situation. Remember Jesus' sacrifice, regardless of the trial. When it comes to making sure we're right with everyone, always wash out the bowl.

- What truth is God communicating to me right now?

- How is God inviting me to respond?

Thursday

GALATIANS 5:16-26

THE PATIENT PATIENT

If we live by the Spirit, let us also keep in step with the Spirit.

GALATIANS 5:25

I DECIDED TO TRY OUT a new doctor not long ago. I had used the same doctor for years. After I read through the New Patient form in the new office, I remembered why I had stuck with the same doctor for so many years.

Somewhere around page 47, I had to consult myancestry.com to provide my family's medical history from four generations back. When I finally finished, my hand was numb and I had to go back and add a new condition.

Then came the real wait.

I looked around and realized the doctor had a great practice. His new digs were posh and well appointed, and his waiting room was full of sick folks. As I thumbed through my fourth or fifth magazine, I noticed the door swing open and heard my name. The nurse weighed me and walked me back to the exam room as I muttered about my weight again.

And then it happened. The nurse lied to me—just flat lied to me. She said, "The doctor will be with you in a moment."

I know she was just being courteous and professional, but why even bother? I went to the room at age 40, and the doctor walked in when I was 52.

I don't know about you, but I can get really impatient sometimes. We live in a microwave society. We want what we want and we want it now!

My patience is tested when another car cuts me off or when I have to wait on a doctor. But Galatians 5:22 gives us a daily litmus test. It's a list of the fruit of the Spirit, and patience is one of the nine traits that will always be present in some measure in someone indwelled by the Holy Spirit.

As you go through your day, run the race with patience, enduring the trials that will come, however small or great they may be.

Many consider patience as a "passive waiting" or "tolerance." But since the New Testament was originally written in Greek, it's best to dive into the Greek to research the real meanings of the words. I learned that most Greek words for patience are active and robust words. So, God intends for us to go about his business while anticipating his perfect answers and direction in his perfect time. He is the perfect doctor who is performing perfect surgery on us. Each of us should endeavor to be his patient patient.

Hebrews 12:1 uses the imagery of running a race with patience. Do people run races passively or tolerantly? Hardly. People run races to win. The word "patience" in this verse is translated "endurance." The patience God prescribes for us means persevering toward a goal, enduring trials, or waiting for a promise to be fulfilled.

As you go through your day, run the race with patience, enduring the trials that will come, however small or great they may be. Strive for the goal to be like Jesus as you wait on Him to fulfill his promise to complete the work He's begun in you (Philippians 1:6).

- What truth is God communicating to me right now?

- How is God inviting me to respond?

Friday

2 PETER 1:3-11

THE CONVENIENCE OF INGRATITUDE

His divine power has granted to us all things that pertain to life and godliness.

2 PETER 1:3

DON'T YOU HATE IT when you get all settled down to watch TV—shirt comfortably in place, feet kicked up, blanket tucked tight, and snack in hand—and you look up to see the remote control on top of the TV?

That's when you need a remote to get the remote.

Do little nuisances like that irritate you? They bother me too much. I'm lazy, so I struggle with most inconveniences. It seems like they come one after another. Just like one man's trash is another man's treasure, one man's nuisance is another man's opportunity. Each time a frustration flares up, I'm learning to try to be thankful for those little inconveniences.

God can teach us to be thankful for even our annoyances. Life has a way of stretching us, and some of us know more about stretch marks than others. The key is our attitudes. Every time something doesn't go our way, we can let it be a stigma or a stimulus. It's up to us.

Instead of grumbling about having to get back up out of the recliner, I'm thankful that I have a TV to watch and a remote that controls it. Instead of fussing about all the traffic,

I'm grateful to live in a metropolitan area that has a lot of places to go and people to meet. Instead of wringing my hands over my car repair bill, I'm thrilled I have a usually reliable way to get where I need to go.

Philippians 2:14 reminds us to, "Do all things without grumbling or disputing, that you may be blameless and innocent." Life is largely made up of little things. An old saying goes, "If Jesus is not the Lord of the little things in your life, then he's not Lord at all." It's easy to thank God for the big blessings and run to him in the big challenges. But how authentic are you in the daily grind, the menial routine of everyday life? Oswald Chambers writes, "Drudgery is one of the finest tests to determine the genuineness of our character."[9]

It's easy to thank God for all the big blessings and run to him in the big challenges. But how authentic are you in the daily grind, the menial routine of everyday life?

God's divine power has granted us everything that pertains to life and godliness. Life is mostly drudgery, but godliness is commanded throughout. Today, make every effort to add to your faith virtue, knowledge, self-control, steadfastness, godliness, brotherly affection, and love.

That's God's way of telling us to have a good attitude.

- What truth is God communicating to me right now?

- How is God inviting me to respond?

ROMANS 5:1-6

THE RACE

I press on toward the goal for the prize of the upward call of God in Christ Jesus.
PHILIPPIANS 3:14

During my shows, I like to ask how many people in the audience exercise. Then I ask how many of them are runners. Usually, a lot of hands go up. Most of those people are under 20.

I remember one guy said his regular exercise regimen had him scheduled to run 20 miles the next day. I looked at him in part admiration and part confusion.

"You know," I said, "They have a thing called an automobile. And you can ride in it."

Can you imagine running that far? I mean, I run every single day. I run from the bathroom back to the bed at least twice. I have an aunt who has run 10 miles a day for the last 10 years. We don't know where she is.

I'm obviously not big on jogging, but the times I've tried started out tough only to get a lot better once I hit my stride.

"Do you not know that in a race all the runners run, but only one receives the prize? So run that you may obtain it" (1 Corinthians 9:24).

You've heard it said that the Christian life is a marathon, not a sprint. But I believe it's more like a steeplechase. Actually, it's a steeplechase on a Cross Country course. The steeplechase is a race that forces runners over hurdles and pitfalls full of water. It is incredibly exhausting with all of the extra challenges.

Today's reading passage assures us that through Jesus Christ we stand in a grace that will sustain us through whatever comes our way. It is super-abounding grace that outlasts sin in our hearts or any force in hell or on Earth. Through that grace, we can rest in the certainty that our Savior is victorious. We know how the story is going to end.

So take heart. You can be thankful in your sufferings because you know that through Jesus you're going to overcome them some day. Know that your trials produce endurance, which produces character, which produces hope. That hope is as sure and steadfast as Jesus himself. May he be the anchor of your soul.

Run the race well, friends. We know who's already won.

"I have said these things to you, that in me you may have peace. In the world you will have tribulation. But take heart; I have overcome the world" (John 16:33).

- What truth is God communicating to me right now?

- How is God inviting me to respond?

References

1. Derek Thomas, *Creation Ex-Nihilo*, https://www.ligonier.org/learn/articles/creation-ex-nihilo/

2. Franklin D. Roosevelt, *1933 Presidential Inaugural Address*, http://historymatters.gmu.edu/d/5057

3. Dictionary.com, *definition of "all,"* http://www.dictionary.com/browse/all?s=t

4. R.C. Sproul, *What Does Inspiration Mean in 2 Timothy 3:16?*, https://www.youtube.com/watch?v=Lcca3pTlm58

5. Ray Comfort, *The Atheist Delusion,* https://www.youtube.com/watch?v=AC5PzoXxRc0&t=259s

6. Oswald Chambers, *My Utmost For His Highest*, February 18 devotional, (Grand Rapids, MI: Discover House Publishers, 1994).

7. John Piper, *Be Filled with the Spirit*, https://www.desiringgod.org/messages/be-filled-with-the-spirit

8. *ESV Study Bible*, Note on John 10:10, Page 2043, (Wheaton, IL: Crossway Bibles, 2008).

9. Chambers, *My Utmost For His Highest*, February 19 devotional, (Grand Rapids, MI: Discover House Publishers, 1994).

NOTE: All stories involving my wife, Donna, were used with the express written permission of Donna herself. Well…most of them.

Acknowledgments

Since this is a devotional, the first Person I should thank is Christ. He is the Logos, the Word, and this book is full of Scripture to help us apply God's principles and glorify him with our lives. Thank you, Jesus, for your love for us and for giving us your precious Word.

Thanks to Eagle's Landing First Baptist Church, Pastor Tim Dowdy, and my entire church family for always pouring into me so I can pour into others.

A special acknowledgment goes to NewLifeRadio.fm and its former morning show host, Pete Chagnon. He encouraged me to do a radio show called *The Monday Mood Changer*, heard on stations throughout the U.S. and webcast worldwide. Those devotional thoughts birthed the idea for this book.

It's always a joy to work with Jason Chatraw and his Ampelon Publishing team. Thanks to Jason for the guidance and book layout, and thanks to Joy Neal for her skillful editing.

Thanks to Spencer Watson for his cover design and Michie Turpin for the cover photos. These guys are rarely in the spotlight but are masterful at their crafts.

Finally, I cannot thank enough my friend and co-author Tim Luke. Tim is a prolific writer and a pastor who loves God's Word and people. Thanks for making these books happen.

For more individual copies or bulk orders
of *I Am Not My Own*, please visit
www.ScottDavis.com/shop or
www.LifeSongPublishing.com.

Also from Scott Davis with Tim Luke:

If My Body Is a Temple, Then I Was a Megachurch